G000095282

the naked i

Authenticity:
Be You, Be Happy

Mark Newey

Published by
Authenticity Publishing

First print run printed and bound by CPI Antony Rowe, Bumpers Farm Industrial Estate, Chippenham, Wiltshire SN14 6LH

Second Print run July 2014 printed and bound in India by Replika Press Pvt Ltd, India

First published in 2013 by Authenticity Publishing
2nd Print run July 2014

Cover Design: www.sharpcreative.co.uk

Back Cover Photography: www.markbourdillon.com

Typesetting: www.als-designs.co.uk

ISBN 978-0-9927104-0-8

Dedication

To each and every one of my clients over the years who had the courage to face their demons however big or small and from whom I have learned so much. This book wouldn't exist without you!

Thank You!

The Secret to Life

Be who you are and say what you feel

Because those who matter don't mind

And those who mind don't matter.

Dr Seuss

Acknowledgements

Firstly I'd like to thank my NLP teachers, especially Ian McDermott who had a huge effect on me at a very crucial part of my life, and also the wonderful Robert Dilts, Suzi Smith, Tim Halbom and Jan Elfline. Also Art Giser for his more spiritual approach through Energetic NLP.

I would also like to thank Brene Brown for her Authenticity, Vulnerability, Honesty and Inspiration. I look forward to meeting her one day!

Thanks too to Dr David Hamilton and the participants on his Self Love workshop in which I made a huge personal discovery which necessitated re-writing part of the book!

I would like to thank Faithless (Maxi Jazz, Sister Bliss, Rollo and Jamie Catto); your music played a major part in my healing and continues to inspire me every day.

I would also like to thank Lis Goodwin, from whom I've learnt so much, for her Openness, Vulnerability, Wisdom and Care through her Kesia Technique ©, Christiane Bergob for her Care, Wisdom and Teaching through Body Psychotherapy and Mary Ellis for her Wisdom and Teaching through Spiritual Coaching, all of whom have had an impact on the content of this book.

A book is never complete without others to look at it!

Huge thanks to my editor Caroline whose left brained focus has dramatically tidied up and sharpened the right brained manuscript I sent to her!

I would like to thank "My Boys": Ade, David and Paul for reminding me what my own book was actually about at a very crucial stage when I was getting myself sidetracked! Also David for being a wonderfully creative, caring and patient graphic designer for me over the years and designing the cover.

I would also like to thank my lovely friend Jane for her continuous support and characteristically incisive feedback.

Finally I'd like to thank my family:

My Dad, for whom I've developed a huge admiration rather late in life!

My Mum who I miss terribly and who never got to see the 'alternative me', but undoubtedly sowed the seeds.

My brother, Paul, who's always a timely and dependable rock.

And of course to my wonderful girls, Vicki, Alex, Jasmine and Antonia for bringing light to my life, especially during the dark times and bearing with me over a rather extended mid-life crisis!

the naked i

Contents

Prologue:
Why this book?

> *"Authenticity is living life from the truth of who you are."*
>
> **Mark Newey**

It's not difficult to see that many, many people are suffering emotionally around you; indeed the very reason that you have picked up this book is because you too are not as happy as you know you could be. Stress, anxiety and even depression are rife, even though we are wealthier (in the West!) than we've ever been. Something's wrong! Something's missing! More and more people are waking up to the fact that there should be more to life. The symptoms of these feelings for most people are a mixture of stress, anxiety and depression.

If you could have consciously sorted your happiness out, you'd have already done it, you wouldn't be reading these words. The problem is that stress (and anxiety and depression) are a simply a tap on your shoulder from your Unconscious to tell you to change something in your life. Stress, anxiety and depression are not mental illnesses; you don't catch them like a disease! They are simply the effect of not living your life in a way that makes you happy. Unfortunately their creation is unconscious and because it's unconscious we don't know what it is we need to change.

This book is about understanding how you've created your stress, what it's trying to tell you and what to do about it. *the naked i* is your guide to changing your life and unlike normal self help books, it does give you the understanding and the tools to go and do it... and keep doing it!

The book's objective is simple: to help you learn how your Mind works and probably for the first time allow yourself to gain real Self Awareness, a real understanding of who you are and why you behave the way you do. With this understanding you can accept yourself, be happy with who you are and JUST BE YOU. This is the secret path to a happier, richer life.

Self Awareness and Self Esteem are the only real answers to stress, anxiety and depression. We need to strip off all those inauthentic layers of "emotional clothing" that we've borrowed from others over the years to protect ourselves: it is these layers of masks and armour that are preventing us from living a happy and rewarding life. Only by revealing the power and beauty of our real selves can we be happy and that means giving up the addiction of worrying about what everybody else thinks.

So why me?

First of all I would like to tell you a little about myself and how I gained the unique knowledge that I'm about to pass on to you. After a relatively successful career working for large multi-national corporates in international marketing, I had an emotional breakdown in 2000. Rather than going on anti-depressants, I got myself out of the 'mind fog' by training in the neurosciences, initially in Neuro-linguistic Programming (NLP), hypnotherapy and Life and Business Coaching. This knowledge gave me a very different way of looking at things. This book can do the same for you!

Having got myself out of the mess I was in, I realised I would be in a good position to help those in similar circumstances. So in 2001, I set up a Neuro-linguistic Psychotherapy practice, called Winning Minds. In the intervening years, I am privileged to have seen literally thousands of one to one clients and helped them deal not only with stress, anxiety and depression, but also a multitude of other issues such as eating disorders, lack of confidence, fears and phobias and food, alcohol, drug and cigarette addictions.

This learning, my own experience and my ongoing research and investigations into the Mind, have given me extensive knowledge in how we, as human beings, create our reality. Since the vast majority of the human mind is unconscious, I have had to find a way of helping people discover their own unconscious emotional and habitual programmes. In other words, I've helped people bring into consciousness what was previously unconscious for them.

To do this, I have created a model (The Mind Matrix ©) through which I take each of my clients so that we can find out the source of their problem and how it manifests in their life. For many of my clients this is sufficient. Once they've discovered how and why they are making themselves stressed, depressed or anxious, they can quickly make the necessary changes in their lives. Obviously, if a client's issues run deeper, they will need further assistance in terms of more formal therapy.

Recently I had one of those earth shattering lightbulb moments! I don't need to be a therapist! I realised that for a huge number of my clients, the conscious understanding of what their unconscious mind was doing was enough for them to sort their lives out.

My passion now is to get this unbelievably powerful information out to as wide an audience as possible to

empower people to transform their own lives! Most people, for whom life is not working, don't need a therapist; they need a way of stepping off life's treadmill and working out what's wrong and what to do about it. That's what this book, *the naked i* is. It's an extremely powerful Self Empowerment tool.

It is not about improving your life... making it better. That's not good enough. That's what most self help books do; they teach you conscious strategies to manipulate yourself into feeling better. This is not a self help book. It's about empowerment and transformation, not the same thing at all. This book will not give you the answers! It's far more powerful than that. It guides you to find **your own** answers.

Some of you will have read other self help books making similarly outrageous claims, but this book **is** different! Well I would say that, wouldn't I?! When you understand the Happiness Hierarchy © and the Mind Matrix © you'll see what I mean. Living Authentically is an ongoing process. It's a life journey.

Please note however that the book is not an alternative to therapy. Those with severe or chronic stress, anxiety or depression will undoubtedly need to see a therapist to move on completely. However, the book will give these people an understanding of how they are creating the reality they don't want and so be of some considerable help.

The crucial understanding that the last ten years have given me, is that the reason the vast majority of people are unhappy, is not because they are ill, but because they are not living their life in a way that actually makes them happy. They are not living authentically. Therapy is not necessary to overcome this, just understanding.

My personal mission is to act as a catalyst for change and enlightenment in the world, by leading and inspiring people to a purer, happier, more respectful, more authentic life. This book is a natural next step in delivering my unique knowledge to a wider audience.

You're about to go on an extraordinary journey that, if you let it, can totally change the direction of your life. It's completely up to you what you do with the understanding you'll get, but providing you take action, your life will never be the same again! Enjoy the ride and remember there is no final destination!

Just Be You,

Mark
Arkesden, England, July 2013

Chapter 1:

The Happiness Hierarchy ©

> *"Only the truth of who you are, if realized, will set you free."*
>
> **Eckhart Tolle**

An important part in all of my clients moving forward over the last ten years has been identifying what they want out of life.

Recently, I went through every single client's notes over the last ten years to work out what the common answers were, i.e. what most people want. Allowing for people using slightly different words, the answers were amazingly consistent - pretty much everybody wants the following:

• To be happy

• To be fulfilled

• To be me (myself)

So how do we get happiness, fulfilment, success and to be ourselves? This is what The Happiness Hierarchy © is all about and I believe that only by consciously going through this process will you be able to empower yourself.

The Happiness Hierarchy © (as depicted in the diagram on page 8) is very different to most self help models because they tend to miss out Step 1 (Self Awareness) and many don't even talk about Step 2 (Self Acceptance). Well, you

The Happiness Hierarchy ©

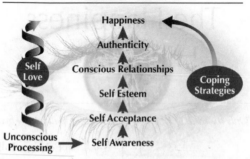

Happiness

Authenticity

Conscious Relationships

Self Love

Self Esteem

Self Acceptance

Unconscious Processing → Self Awareness

Coping Strategies

can't have happiness, fulfilment and success unless you have Self Esteem (feeling good about yourself); you can't have Self Esteem without Self Acceptance; you can't have Self Acceptance without Self Awareness; you can't have Self Awareness unless you understand what is going on in your unconscious mind. And you can't have any of this unless you love yourself!

The unconscious mind is a topic that for some reason most people are too scared to tackle! Our unconscious is actually 91% of our overall Mind; the Conscious Mind (the bit we're aware of!) is just 9%. In fact, scientists struggle to agree on an exact percentage, but 9% versus 91% is a conservative estimate.

Most self help books teach you rational, logical strategies to help you try and manipulate your behaviour and your mindset so that you can cope and therefore feel better. This is represented by the long arrow on the far right of The Happiness Hierarchy © diagram above.

Rational, logical strategies always require a lot of willpower which requires conscious thought ("I mustn't eat that biscuit"). Our conscious mind represents just

9% of our overall mind, and since the vast majority of our issues are unconscious (otherwise we'd have sorted them out!), teaching conscious strategies to manipulate behaviour and mindset cannot be a long term solution to Self Empowerment.

I should point out that the model is only a guideline rather than a fixed, rigid route to happiness. It doesn't mean that you tick off each level as you go up and that's you sorted for the rest of your life! It also shouldn't be taken to mean that this is the route in every part of your life. In some areas of our life we already have Self Esteem, even without proper Self Awareness - but very few of us have it across the board! If you keep Authenticity, via Self Esteem, Self Acceptance and Self Awareness in your mind as your Map towards Happiness, it means that you've always got something to aim for, especially when times are tough and you're not feeling good.

The Starting Point: Self Love

Self Love is the single most important ingredient for our journey towards happiness and I nearly missed it completely! In fact it has been a huge blind spot for me my whole life, I just wasn't aware of it. I attended a workshop given by Dr David Hamilton called "I Heart Me: The Science of Self Love". I'd heard of David and this was a topic that seemed to be close to what I was writing about, so I thought I'd attend.

About two hours in, I nearly fell off my chair (literally!). I asked if Self Love and Self Esteem weren't just different words for the same thing. David simply pointed out that it was perfectly possible to feel good about yourself (Self Esteem) because of your achievements and still not love yourself..." Boom!" Right bang where I was in my life!

I have developed a healthy level of Self Esteem, after picking myself up from my breakdown and helping so many others get their lives back on track too, but did I love myself? No, not really. I have to own up to being in tears on the train journey home! It had never occurred to me that I could simply love myself.

I came back to the third session four weeks later and whilst I was just beginning to get the hang of it, I just couldn't fit Self Love into The Happiness Hierarchy © model. But if I haven't had it in my life, that's not surprising. I couldn't work out whether it should come in before Self Acceptance, Self Esteem or Authenticity in the Hierarchy. So I asked the other 50 workshop attendees and I got a very clear answer: "Self Love is the whole thing - it's all-encompassing and it's what allows us to go up the Hierarchy." Thanks guys, I've got it now!

In many ways, it just takes a single conscious decision that we can love ourselves no matter what. Then it's a case of continually reminding ourselves until we've overridden the old "useless, worthless, hopeless" neural pathways we've developed over the years and the Self Love becomes hardwired in. David taught us many brilliant exercises and techniques to do this, but my favourite is the simplest. **Every** time I look in the mirror, I smile at myself and tell myself "I love you" and what's more I now mean it!

We're all going to have different ideas as to what Self Love is, but I would say the primary ingredient is Self Compassion. At one time or another, we've all been stupid, nasty, pathetic, boring, unsupportive, perhaps even useless! But none of that means that we can't love ourselves. Self Love is about "being there" for ourselves 24 hours a day even when - or even especially when - we've messed up! But most of us will "beat ourselves up" for being stupid, nasty, pathetic, boring, unsupportive, perhaps even useless!

Unless you're a raving axe murderer, we all have the right to love ourselves regardless of what we have or haven't done, regardless of what others think of us, regardless of whether we've messed up or not. The difficulty for us Brits is that we've been brought up to think that loving ourselves is narcissistic and egotistical. It's a very unBritish thing to do! Loving yourself is only harmful or offensive if it makes you selfish and upsets other people.

Self Love is a very personal, internal thing: it's not about other people and they don't need to know whether you've got it or not. I dare you to find one good reason why you should not love yourself! If you manage to come up with a reason, when you look at that reason in the cold light of day, I bet it's not valid.

In terms of The Happiness Hierarchy ©, Self Love is both the lubricant and the glue in our journey towards happiness. Self Love helps us to move from Self Awareness to Self Acceptance, from Self Acceptance to Self Esteem and from Self Esteem to Authenticity, the lubricant. It's also what holds everything together including our Sense of Self, the glue.

Step 1: Self Awareness

Step 1 requires us to bring into consciousness what our unconscious is doing, how it's filtering all of that information that comes in every second of the day. We all have very individual filtering processes. The four paragraphs below are a tiny summary of The Mind Matrix © model which explains our filtering process, the full version of which will unfold in Part 1.

Having Self Awareness means knowing how your own personal history and make-up are influenced by the following:

- Your Values

Knowing what is important to you (like honesty, respect, community, sharing) is crucial to understanding yourself and how you create your reality, and therefore how happy you are. If you are not honouring your Values in the way you live your life, you will not feel good about yourself; indeed, you won't be able to be the real "Me" and be happy.

- Childhood Programming

The experiences you had as a child and young adult will stay with you as part of your unconscious filtering process throughout adulthood, as will the influences and teachings of your parents and any other key adults in your life. You need to be aware of what these influences are so that you can leave any negative or undesirable ones behind.

These influences create unconscious programmes when you're young. However, whilst the programming may have been beneficial as a child, it rarely is as an adult. This often means forgiveness for those significant adults in your childhood. They would have been doing the best they could at the time. It may well mean forgiving yourself, too! Dealing with negative personal history will 'clean up' your filtering process dramatically.

- Cultural Programming

Today cultural programming is everywhere and the delivery can be relentless due to the power of modern media like TV and the internet. We tend to give these media an authority and credibility that they don't deserve. We tend to believe what we hear or read as being true.

Cultural programming encourages us to conform to society standards for how we look, how we behave, what makes us happy, what makes us successful.

The chances are that with real Self Awareness, you will start to not conform, you'll just be you. It doesn't mean you'll become antisocial, you just won't be pigeonholed anymore! Funnily enough somebody recently threw 'nonconformist' at me and meant it as an insult. I thought about it for a couple of seconds and then thanked him, explaining that for me it was actually a compliment.

• Beliefs

We all have limiting beliefs about what we can and can't do in our lives. The problem is that because the beliefs are unconscious and we don't know they're there, we think they're true and run our lives accordingly. It's inevitable with the continual comparisons made at school, at work and even amongst our mates (and often with completely inappropriate comparisons like celebrities) that we don't feel good about ourselves. Because most of us don't have the Self Awareness (yet!) we can't correct these beliefs. The exercises in the workbook will help you work out what some of your limiting beliefs are, then – when you hold them up to the light – you can dismiss them as untrue and change your filtering system.

Step 2: Self Acceptance

When you start to gain awareness of who you are, you can begin to accept yourself, warts and all. We will all find that actually we're OK; we're pretty good people! When we have Self Awareness, we can accept all of our vulnerabilities and personal foibles. When we start to understand ourselves we may however find things about ourselves that we don't like. Well now we know what they are, we can do something about them!

Part 1 of the book is about helping you really understand your own personal unconscious programmes and then helping you change what you don't like. There may also be some things that you don't like that you can't change; this may be something that involves your relationships with others (you can't make other people change, no matter how hard you try!) or it may be about how you look. You just have to accept them and move on.

Step 3: Self Esteem

Self Esteem is the bedrock for happiness, fulfilment and success. It means, having accepted who you are, feeling good about yourself, after you've completed Steps 1 and 2. One of the main outcomes for my clients is that their Self Esteem increases dramatically. I often say that when you have Self Esteem, when you feel good about yourself, then your whole world changes. Interestingly nothing changes in the world outside, it all changes in your head. Having Self Esteem fundamentally transforms your filtering process.

There are so many influences (people and society) working against you having Self Esteem that once you learn to have it, you will never let it go. However, you may find those around you, even those close to you, don't like your newfound Self Esteem and will unconsciously fight it and try and rob you of it, because it doesn't fit with their existing model of you. If they don't have Self Esteem themselves, then they may feel threatened by yours.

But that's the whole point about Self Esteem; it doesn't matter what others think. Here's my favourite quotation from the children's story writer, Dr Seuss:

> *"Be who you are and say what you feel, because those who mind don't matter and those who matter don't mind."*

In fact, when people ask me the secret to a happy life, this is it!

Step 4: Conscious Relationships

Contrary to what Western cultural programming would have you believe, money and lots of "stuff" don't make us happy; it's people (and not just close relationships, but all relationships) that make us happy. We have that in common with all animals, but because of the sophistication of our brains, we make relationships much too complicated, unlike animals!

Because of a lack of Self Esteem, most people live in fear: fear of being found out, fear of not living up to people's expectations, fear of not being as good as other people. The Mind Chatter caused by this fear means that most people have a running commentary in their heads about what others are thinking about them. When you have Self Esteem, this all falls away, it becomes irrelevant.

The vast majority of our relationships are shallow and incongruent because we don't share ourselves properly, we hold things back. We hide our vulnerabilities because we're frightened that if people get to see the real 'us', then our survival will be in danger. We put on masks and armour to protect ourselves. This self defence strategy runs unconsciously and automatically. It is very difficult to be 'real' with people when we don't have Self Awareness, Self Acceptance and Self Esteem - we're continually hiding.

Step 5: Authenticity

> **"Authenticity is living life from the truth of who you are."**

The penultimate step on The Happiness Hierarchy © is Authenticity. Authenticity is simple, it's just being **you.** When you have learnt who you are, accepted and begun to love yourself, your relationships (including the one with yourself) will automatically become more rewarding. You can just be you: no masks, no pretence, no manipulation, no hiding.

The liberation from the relentless running commentary in the head is immeasurable. When you can just be you then happiness and fulfilment are round the corner. Success, whatever that means to you, will require some action on your part, but when you are acting authentically, success comes so much more quickly and easily.

Step 6: Happiness, Fulfilment and Success

Follow the previous five steps and you will find what you're looking for. What is more, happiness and fulfilment are not a final destination; they are the journey.

You can see how the so called modern illnesses of Stress, Anxiety and Depression (or S.A.D. as I abbreviate them) prevent us from getting what we want. With Self Awareness and Self Esteem they fall away. Unfortunately, society tends to discourage us from doing the necessary internal searches to begin this process.

In Chapter 10, I will take you through a model that, with your newfound Self Awareness, will help to ensure that you make any changes in your life in the right places. Making them in the wrong places can make things worse!

The model is not meant as a definitive solution to making changes, it's just a simple guideline that allows you to double check what you need to do. Sometimes the changes you want to make will not be totally within your control (for instance, when you want to move to the country and your partner doesn't). Then you have a choice to make and you need to come to terms with the outcome and you may have to make a compromise.

Chapter 2:
What is
The Mind Matrix ©?

> *"Until you make the unconscious conscious, it will direct your life and you will call it fate."*
>
> **Carl Jung**

The Human Mind

Our reality (the way we see the world) is based on our imagination but it's not real! Reality is an illusion!

Ruby Wax explains how this works in her wonderful book, *Sane New World:* "Much of what you see out there is manufactured by your brain, painted in like computer-generated graphics in a movie; only a very small part of the inputs to your occipital lobe comes directly from the external world, the rest comes from internal memory stores and other processes... In actuality we see the world in single snapshots and it is a part of your brain makes it seem like it's constantly moving... Think of *The Wizard of Oz* - you're being run by the guy behind the curtain." [1]

Now that's sunk in, you're thinking I'm stark raving mad and you're about to throw the book in the bin! Hang on, let me explain. I'll give you an example!

You've just been to an interview for a new job and you're pretty confident of getting it. Then a week later you get a very polite letter saying that on this occasion the company will not be pursuing your application any further. You're gutted! You may then have one of a number of different reactions.

Try these two on for size!

1. "It's no good, I'm just not good enough. That's another rejection. I'm useless. I'm just going to have to accept that I'm not going to be able to go any further in my career and knuckle down to a mundane 9.00-5.00 existence where I am."

2. "What a cheek! I'm plenty good enough for that job. They're just blind."

The reality is that they had a candidate who suited their requirements better for that particular job than you did. It is actually no slight on you at all. The above two reactions are simply our **interpretation** of what actually happened. But what becomes our reality? If we're honest with ourselves, most of us have number one as our reality. It's an interpretation, not reality. However, we are doing this in every situation, in every second of our lives. Our life is an interpretation of reality, it's how the human mind works.

So it is absolutely essential to understand what our own unconscious programming is that creates our 'reality'; then we can get closer to the truth and live life without the constant doubt and Mind Chatter.

The difference between humans and other animals is the size of our neocortex (the thinking brain). Its development in early humans increased our adaptability and therefore our ability to survive as a species. We learned faster and were far superior at inventing and reasoning and so were able to outsmart our predators, even though they were vastly bigger, and well equipped with claws and teeth!

It is the neocortex that allows us to invent things and take on new skills and behaviours. It gathers huge amounts of information and then creates models through imagination to explore and solve problems. So in evolutionary terms, we don't have to wait for the normal, long winded Darwinian process, we can change our evolution with new theories and inventions. The neocortex is not just about survival, it also allows us to be creative, to appreciate music, art and literature, to philosophise and dream. It helps us develop our own unique personality.

The human brain is often referred to as the world's most advanced computer processing mechanism, acting as a vast network with huge memory capacity and super high speeds. The number of potential connections within the human brain is virtually unlimited and yet through our evolution, we've managed to pack all of this into something the size of a melon! So why is it that we use such a small amount of the total capacity of our brain? Well in evolutionary terms, Homo Sapiens is a very young species and we're still learning.

If it's so amazing, why is it that we can't use our huge brain to make us happy? Cordelia Fine [2] explores the way the Unconscious deletes and distorts incoming information, sometimes to slightly alarming effect, and shows perfectly what can happen when our filtering system isn't working for us.

"But the truth of the matter is... that your unscrupulous brain is entirely undeserving of your confidence. It has some shifty habits that leave the truth distorted and disguised. Your brain is vainglorious. It's emotional and immoral. It deludes you. It is pigheaded, secretive and weak willed. Oh, and it's also a bigot...That fleshy walnut is all you have in order to know yourself and to know the world. Yet, thanks to the masquerading of an untrustworthy brain with a mind of its own, much of what you think you know is not quite as it seems." Her book is lighthearted, but the problem is that the Unconscious' ability to delete and distort causes us stress, anxiety and depression. All of these unpleasant states of mind are created by our imagination.

Interestingly, with the new scanning technologies developed literally only in the last five to ten years, our understanding of how the mind works is growing at an incredible rate. It is my belief that over the next ten to fifteen years, this will allow us to get to grips with the so called 'mental health' problems with which we seem to be currently inundated. Exciting times!

The problem at the moment is that our mind gets swamped with random thoughts, based on how we are unconsciously processing the information that comes in from the world around us. These thoughts pop up any old time whether we like it or not! So despite the human brain being the world's most advanced computer, we have yet to master the skills of using it to make us happy!

What is The Mind Matrix ©?

The Mind Matrix © is a simple, 'hands on' model of how the human mind works. The Matrix shows us how we create our world, our reality. Most people live their day to day lives under the assumption that there is one world, one version of reality. Well here's a shock, there are seven billion versions. We all create our worlds differently. If we understood and took this one fact to heart in the way we live our lives, there could be a lot less conflict in the world.

Most people are scared to learn about or even talk about the Unconscious. Freud portrayed it as a mass of seething and conflicting programmes. The purpose of The Mind

Matrix © is to present the Unconscious in a simple and non threatening manner. The only way to really understand the model is to compare it with your own experiences and thought patterns. These experiences and thought patterns are your own personal filters for the mass of incoming information every second of the day. This means that each person who studies the generalised model ends up starting to understand their own unconscious patterns.

The Mind Matrix © is therefore a model from which we can become more conscious of the way we experience our unconscious emotional and habitual programmes and how they affect the way we live our lives. From this we can learn how we can all dramatically improve the world we live in, on a personal level and on a societal level, by bringing the Unconscious into Consciousness.

Some of the ideas covered in this chapter may be somewhat controversial to mainstream thought on how the human mind works and how we currently deal with mental health problems, but the objective of developing The Mind Matrix © is not to attack current thinking, but rather to challenge it. The workings of the Matrix are straightforward and by and large unarguable. This chapter sets the background to why we need to radically rethink our attitude and treatment of the Mind.

As a species, we desperately need to understand what is going on inside our heads at a personal level and a societal level. The nature of modern life demands a better understanding for the individual, but particularly for those teaching, managing, leading or helping others. Current Theory of Mind is not readily accessible to the majority of people because the information is overly academic and theoretical and so not readily applicable on a day to day basis. The Mind Matrix © corrects that.

Why is The Mind Matrix © necessary?

Life today in the West is unrecognisable to life even just fifty years ago. If our grandparents or great grandparents were to get a snapshot of life today, they would undoubtedly be in awe of the progress, but terrified by the speed and impersonal nature of the way we live.

However, for those privileged to live in the West, the increase in the incidence of mental health issues (depression, stress, anxiety, eating disorders) has roughly matched the increase in wealth over that half century. So the wealthier we've become, the more depressed we've become!

In the seventies we were being told that computers would allow us all to work a three day week. We would have far more time for leisure and relaxation. Predicting the future cannot be an exact science, but that must be one of the most 'off the mark' predictions ever. Not only are we working longer hours, but there are now signs that the age for retirement could easily go up to seventy from sixty five within the next ten years!

Here are a few things to think about:

- We get more visual and mental stimulation today in **one day** than our grandparents had in **one year**!

- The human brain can no longer keep up with the pace of change

- 80% of visits to the doctor are caused by stress

- 70% of serious disease incidences are caused by stress

So what happened to all the leisure and the three day week? What's gone so badly wrong?

The ethical side of our lives has lagged far, far behind the technical advances. The understanding of the impact of these technical advances on society and culture at large, simply isn't there. We will return to this theme in Chapter 5 when we look at Brain Dominance.

So we do need, as individuals, to understand much more about how we create our own reality. We create S.A.D. through our imagination. Understanding The Mind Matrix © empowers us to make changes in our lives and let go of the S.A.D.

How has The Mind Matrix © been developed?

The structure of the Mind Matrix © is an adaptation of The Meta Model developed by Richard Bandler and John Grinder, the creators of Neuro-linguistic Programming or NLP. It also adapts the S.C.O.R.E model developed by Robert Dilts, another luminary from the NLP world. The Mind Matrix © takes these theoretical models, adds to them and adapts them into a simple, hands on, practical model to explain how the Mind works. Indeed much of the ethos of The Mind Matrix © is taken from NLP.

The further workings of The Mind Matrix © are formed from my own observations and experiences, and those gained from coaching and helping thousands of people to deal with issues such as stress, depression, anxiety, eating disorders, weight loss, smoking and alcohol abuse.

Most traditional psychological theories concerning the Mind tend to be very one dimensional as well as academic and unapproachable. They only take into account the behavioural, genetic, neuro-anatomical, sociological or developmental reasons for a person's thought processes. The Mind Matrix © explains what is going on in an easily identifiable way, taking into account information coming into the brain from the external world, and how we filter it all in our mind. It's a comprehensive look at the human mind that is remarkable because it is not only a generalised model, but allows the individual to tailor make their own personal interpretation.

The Mind Matrix © has made particular impact on clients of mine who are GP's, who feel they can relate at least part of the model to their patients when dealing with stress and depression. It also made an impact on a 3rd year psychology student who came to our offices for some work experience. His comment was: "The Mind Matrix © pulls in a number of existing psychological Theories of Mind into one place and then immediately dismisses the rest of them as unnecessary!"

How does The Mind Matrix © work?

The Mind Matrix ©

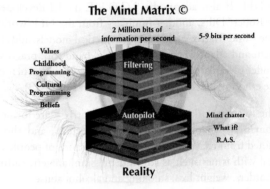

What follows is a brief summary of The Mind Matrix © and how the Mind works, the rest of the book will follow the unconscious information processing in far more detail. The critical factor is that 91% of our Mind is unconscious, a fact of which very few people are aware. In other words, 91% of the way we live our life is unconscious. If you doubt that, have a quick think about the way you drive.

When was the last time you watched yourself purposefully putting your foot on the accelerator? The answer would be when you were still consciously learning how to drive.

Literally 91% of the actions you take are unconscious, which is why you can drive and yet have a complex conversation with a passenger at the same time. In fact, you sometimes pay so little conscious attention to the driving you can arrive at your destination, having no recollection of huge parts of the journey - autopilot! But you have done everything you should have done: changed gear, braked, stopped at traffic lights, indicated to turn left and so on.

Your Unconscious does that for you without you having to consciously think. These actions are so repetitive that you train your Unconscious to do them for you.

📖 Pippa and Charlotte's Story:

Recently, I was explaining this to two clients who were sisters and played very high level tennis. The purpose of their practice sessions was to repetitively play the same shot time after time, after time, after time, after time, to train their Unconscious to play the shot automatically for them.

Once they were on the court in a competition, I forbade them from 'thinking' because when they started thinking, they either talked themselves down and started doubting their ability or got distracted by their thoughts, affecting their performance. They'd practised every type of shot so many times that if they just let their Unconscious get on with it, then they would play most, if not all, of their tennis 'in the flow'.

However, the unconscious programmes can be negative as well as positive. Many 'bad habits' occur around food for example! It doesn't matter how often we tell ourselves (consciously) not to eat chocolate, we end up doing it. In fact, the more we worry about chocolate, the more we end up eating. Dieting is based on willpower. Since you have to think to use willpower, it resides in your conscious Mind.

Willpower is one of the most overrated of human capacities. The reason diets never work is that somebody is using 9% of their conscious Mind to overcome the (incorrect) programming that a bar of chocolate will make us feel better, which lies in the Unconscious (91%).

Huge developments in the neurosciences are taking place; no longer are we hidebound by the mantra of the eighties and nineties that genetics explain everything about us. We used to think that you couldn't develop new brain cells: you had what you were born with; your brain was hard wired. Well it's not! It's soft wired! Your brain has plasticity; its wiring can change with experience and learning. Genes set up our potential, but they do not control our thoughts, our feelings or our behaviour.

In fact, the wiring is changing all the time, each time we remember something new. By making connections between different ideas, we also make wiring connections that encode those ideas in our brain. A memorable phrase often used in neuroscience circles is "cells that fire together, wire together", it aptly describes what happens in your brain when you have new experiences and learning. The more you take a particular action (e.g. practising your forehand at tennis), the more the particular brain cells fire together, the stronger the connection becomes, and the more easily you take the action in the future. This is great news for those who feel that their life isn't what it should be, who are sad, anxious, stressed. We can change our brain's wiring! [3]

The Mind Matrix ©

The starting point for The Mind Matrix © is that your total body/mind system can take in two million bits of information a second which is an almost unquantifiable amount. In fact, there is no universally agreed figure, but two million is a very conservative and widely accepted figure. Importantly though, according to cognitive psychologist, George Miller, the conscious mind can only deal with five to nine bits of information at any one time. [4]

The big question is: what happens to the other one million, nine hundred and ninety-nine thousand nine hundred and ninety-three bits of information that we remain totally unaware of? How an individual's mind deals with the incoming information creates that person's own individual Map of the World, a concept we will be revisiting throughout the book. Everyone has a different Map of the World.

The mind then uses an unconscious filtering system, every second of the day to deal with the incoming mass of information, much of which is instantly deleted (i.e. you are not aware of what you're deleting). For example, you only become aware of the big toe on your right foot when I ask you how it feels. It's there all the time, but it's of very little relevance the vast majority of the time, even when you're walking on it.

The unconscious filtering system decides what is relevant and what isn't. If the information fits with a particular unconscious programme, it will fire up that programme unconsciously. The filtering system triggers the generalised programming which we then dutifully run, without being able to consider whether it is productive or not.

The programming then activates the relevant behaviour. If the behaviour is negative or unwanted, then a negative emotion is tagged with it (anger, guilt, shame, anxiety). The negative emotion can then lead to more unconscious behavioural programming, followed by more negative emotional programming and the pattern repeats itself, eventually creating stress or depression.

Stress, anxiety and depression (S.A.D.) are all 'in the mind', they don't actually exist. This isn't to say that the person isn't suffering, it's just that the suffering isn't real. Indeed, the definition of stress is the perceived inability to cope with the demands being made on us. The key word is *perceived*, because the person sat at the desk next door to us at work can have exactly the same demands being made on them, but cope admirably. They have simply filtered the two million bits of incoming information differently.

Many of us use coping mechanisms for getting through the stressful nature of modern life. These coping mechanisms then easily become habits or addictions: smoking, booze, comfort eating, coffee. The trouble is none of them work. In fact, if anything, we cope even less when we get trapped by the 'bad' habits.

This inevitably results in **Mind Chatter** - that nagging voice in the head that's telling us we're useless, we can't do this or that, the world's a nasty, dangerous place and so on. The Mind Chatter then gets us into **negative hallucinations** about what might happen if this, if that, what we can and can't do etc.

The continuous Mind Chatter and negative hallucination, which are active in the background all day long and very repetitive, inevitably begin to unconsciously focus our Minds on what they are chattering or hallucinating about, so that we notice things that confirm the chatter or hallucination. "There you see, I knew I couldn't catch it", as we drop the ball! The part of the Mind that looks for the confirmation is called the **reticular activating system (RAS).** The RAS has a huge impact on what information gets focussed on or deleted as the incoming information hits the filtering stage and is of course completely unconscious.

The whole process is unconscious and is therefore difficult to change, particularly if we haven't learnt what the process is, i.e. it's not consciously available to us. Learning the process (allowing it to become consciously available) through The Mind Matrix © results in us being a long way down the path to having more control.

The Mind Matrix © allows us to understand how we are creating our particular reality so that we can do something about it by consciously changing the way we look at things and making conscious lifestyle changes. Deeper issues will require professional assistance, but a lot of my clients can begin the 'recovery process' on their own by making the conscious changes. So the earlier somebody learns, understands and takes control of their own Mind Matrix ©, then the earlier they can solve their own issues.

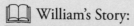 William's Story:

William was a classic case of somebody bringing a particular problem (symptom) but the solution being something seemingly only loosely related and quite unexpected. This is the Unconscious we're dealing with!

After being a salesman for an IT-related company where he was making presentations frequently, William set up his own company. Despite ten very successful years, with the company growing year on year and taking on more and more employees, he came to me with a fear of making presentations. The more senior the person he was presenting to, the worse the anxiety. In some instances he would have to excuse himself to go to the toilet as he felt so sick.

As we started to unpack what was happening, he realised it wasn't every single presentation, as he thought it was. He felt that the presentations he was giving to companies on his buying trips to China were much easier as things easily "got lost in translation"! However, what was really happening here was that he was the buyer and not the seller: they had to sell to him.

To his surprise we also then found out that once a relationship had been made with the person, further presentations were not a problem. In fact, over 70% of their clients had been with them for all of the ten years. At this point, we realised that the reason for his company's success was all about relationships; as a company they really listened and worked with their customers. William decided there and then to reprint his business card and call himself Relationship Director, to make the point.

He then realised that the reason he was nervous on the first presentation was that so much was riding on that first meeting. So we talked through a strategy for these meetings and decided that after a one minute introduction to his company, which was all that was needed to establish credibility as a supplier due to their amazing track record, he would be open and vulnerable and explain in advance why he got so nervous. However, immediately he'd given himself permission to be nervous, the nerves went!

The realisation that he was in the "people business" every bit as much as the semi-conductor business has transformed the future strategy for running the business: a completely unexpected outcome and actually more important than his apparent fear of making presentations.

My dream is to get this knowledge as far and wide as possible so that people don't need to see a therapist, they can live a more fulfilling life on their own. A passion of mine is to get The Mind Matrix © recognised as part of the school curriculum. If a teenager can understand how their Mind works, they have far more chance of growing up to be a more confident and open minded adult. A new generation of children with this knowledge would undoubtedly change the world.

Chapter 3:
See, Hear, Feel, Smell, Taste

> *"You don't need eyes to see, you need vision."*
>
> **Maxi Jazz, Faithless**

The Mind Matrix ©

The first filter of The Mind Matrix © is our senses. We have five senses: visual, auditory, kinaesthetic (feeling), olfactory and gustatory. For the purposes of keeping the model simple, we will discount the last two. Relatively little of the two million bits of information come through smell or taste; information coming through our noses or mouths tends to be situation specific around food!

That leaves us with the focus on sight, hearing and feeling. Whilst we naturally do all three of these – unless of course we are blind or deaf, in which case the mind compensates as best as it can – most people have a bias towards one of the remaining senses. In other words, we have a preferred processing mechanism. NLP refers to these as representational systems (or rep systems for short).

Our Unconscious contains a massive amount of information. In fact, everything we've ever seen, heard, felt, smelt or tasted since we were babies. On a day to day basis, most of the information we need to analyse or to think something through, is there in the unconscious mind, we just have to find it. But the senses use different routes to find the information and bring it into consciousness.

So imagine that you and I are having a nice chat, and that you've said something to me that I don't immediately understand and I have to think about it. Depending on whether I am mainly visual, auditory or kinaesthetic, I will use a different strategy to recall the information from the Unconscious to understand what you are saying to me.

Visual

If my preferred processing mechanism is visual, what actually happens is that my eyes go up towards the ceiling, (see diagram 2.1 and 2.2 below) as I'm searching for the information in the back of my head. In my Unconscious, in a split second, I am playing a 'film' of the memory of an experience I've had or perhaps something I've seen on TV or at the cinema. I'm looking for the information visually, although I'm not consciously aware of that.

Interestingly my eyes will move to different sides, depending on whether I'm imagining or remembering the information. If the eyes go up and to my left, then I'm remembering something that I've already seen, in other words a memory. This is called visual recall in NLP. For example, if you asked me what colour my front door is, I'd make a picture of it in my Mind, but because the door actually exists, I'd be remembering it. (Diagram 2.1)

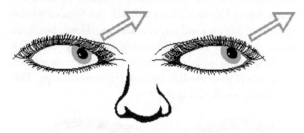

Visual Recall
(Diagram 2.1)

If I'm imagining something, then my eyes go up and to my right; this is called visual construct. So for example, if you asked me what my front door would look like if it was painted a different colour, my eyes would go to my right.

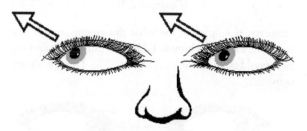

Visual Construct
(Diagram 2.2)

The eye movement (or accessing cues in NLP) happen in a split second as I locate the relevant information to understand what you've just said.

Auditory

If my primary processing mechanism is listening, then my Mind will do something slightly different in order to locate the information. I'm listening in the back of my head to a conversation I've had, the soundtrack to a film, or a radio broadcast. My eyes will stay at a horizontal level, but again go to the left if I'm remembering something. So if I'm thinking about what noise the engine of my car makes, my eyes will go to the left, because I'm remembering. This is auditory recall. (Diagram 2.3)

Auditory Recall
(Diagram 2.3)

However, if you asked me what the engine sounds like when the exhaust is blown, I'd have to imagine it and my eyes would go to the right. (Diagram 2.4). This is auditory construct.

Auditory Construct
(Diagram 2.4)

Kinaesthetic (feeling)

If, on the other hand, my preferred processing mechanism is my feelings, then my eyes will do something different again. The eyes will go down towards the floor and to my right. (Diagram 2.5) This counts as external feeing (touch) or internal feeling (feelings or emotions). Interestingly, my eyes go to the right whether I'm remembering a feeling or imagining it. This is because I'm feeling with my gut, how I felt in a similar situation to the one you are talking about in our chat, to understand what you're saying now.

Kinaesthetic
(Diagram 2.5)

If I'm not sure which sense or rep system to use or I'm not sure what information I'm looking for, my eyes will go down to the right. (Diagram 2.6) This is referred to as an internal dialogue in NLP.

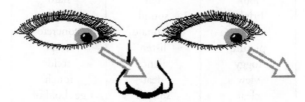

Internal Dialogue
(Diagram 2.6)

Once I know what information I need, then my eyes will go back to the preferred eye accessing cues.

Some people actually reverse the lateral direction their eyes travel. In other words, if they are imagining what something looks like, their eyes will go to the left and not the right, and vice versa if they are remembering something. However, for the vast majority of people, the above rules apply in terms of how they access information. NLP practitioners learn to pick up somebody's preferred processing mechanism by watching the person's eye accessing cues; it takes some practice and concentration though!

Interestingly, our preferred processing mechanism also comes out in our language. The way we think will dictate the words we choose to describe something. If we are mainly visual, our language will be full of visual words and phrases. If we are mainly auditory, then we will use different words to describe the same thing. In NLP terminology, these are called language predicates or just predicates. Below is a table that splits example predicates up into visual, auditory and kinaesthetic.

Visual	Auditory	Kinaesthetic
see	hear	feel
look	tell	hard
bright	sound	unfeeling
clear	resonate	concrete
picture	listen	scrape
foggy	silence	solid
view	deaf	touch
clear	squeak	get hold of
focused	hush	catch on
dawn	roar	tap into
reveal	melody	heated argument

illuminate	make music	pull some strings
imagine	harmonise	sharp as a tack
hazy	tune in/out	smooth operator
an eyeful	rings a bell	make contact
short-sighted	quiet as a mouse	throw out
sight for sore	voiced an	firm foundation
eyes	opinion	get a handle on
take a peek	clear as a bell	get in touch
tunnel vision	give me your ear	with
bird's eye view	loud and clear	hand in hand
naked eye	purrs like	hang in there
paint a picture	a kitten	grasp
	on another note	

For more information on eye accessing cues and language predicates, please see *Frogs into Princes* by Richard Bandler and John Grinder, the developers of NLP: details are in the Resources Section.

Thus, with our very first filter, our own different bias towards the representational systems, we interpret incoming information differently to others. So for example; we've all had the experience of going to the cinema with a friend, seeing the same film and therefore receiving identical input, but wondering if it was the same film, when we compare notes as we walk out! "How did they get that? I didn't get that!" Even with the first filter we see the world differently to others, we create our own reality!

Chapter 4:
OK, What's Really Important?

> *"Your beliefs become your thoughts,*
> *Your thoughts become your words,*
> *Your words become your actions,*
> *Your actions become your habits,*
> *Your habits become your values,*
> *Your values become your destiny."*
>
> **Mahatma Ghandi**

The Mind Matrix ©

The next filter, through which the two million bits of information per second go, is our Values. Values are what is important to us in our lives.

So if I asked you to think of the five most important things to you in your life, what would you come up with? Probably your family, friends, house, job, dog! Whilst they're important, they're not Values. Values, by definition, are intangible; you can't touch them. You can touch your family, your house etc.

So Values are things like honesty, integrity, justice, responsibility, passion, being nonjudgemental. Values are somewhat esoteric words that we throw into our language without really thinking about what they mean and how powerful they are in creating our reality.

We actually make decisions on the basis of our Values every second of the day, without thinking! So if I asked you now to write down, 'off the top of your head', your top five Values, could you do it? When I pose this to my clients, most answer "No"; the best they can do is to conjure up two or three if I give them a moment or two, but that's it. Shouldn't we know what's important to us in our lives? Isn't it essential to know what these important unconscious filtering concepts are? They have a massive impact on how we create our reality.

And yet out of the thousands of one to one clients I've seen, not one has been able to get to five quickly, because none of us has thought about it. Interestingly, those whose minds don't go completely blank and who come up with a few, find that these are the most obvious Values, but not necessarily the most important ones.

When we start to develop a sense of what we want from life, then it's essential we do a bit of planning. We wouldn't just set off in the car if we wanted to get from one end of the country to the other and our life's journey is much more important than a single car journey! Why do people just get on the treadmill and expect their life to work out?

In the workbook there are simple exercises to help you find out what your most important Values are - the real ones, not the most obvious ones! It then guides you to put a score to those Values, in order to demonstrate to what degree they exist in your life. If you are one of the many people who is dissatisfied with your life, you'll find that you are violating your Values. If you have low Values scores, then pay attention! In order to be happy, you must honour your Values. In fact, if you have low scores, you must find a way of bringing those Values into your life as you won't be happy until you have. Finding out what your Values are will give you signposts for improving your life.

With my one to one clients who come for depression, I often find that virtually all their scores are low. They have to find a way to bring all of those things into their life as part of the process of moving out of depression. With stressed clients most of the scores are reasonable and then one or two are very low. Again pay attention! There's a clue or two there!

And remember your Values affect your automated, unconscious thinking every second of the day. Have you ever instantly got really upset about something somebody has said or done? You suddenly became really angry or burst into tears. You then stood back and said to yourself:"I think I might have over reacted. Where did all that come from?" The chances are that somebody absolutely stamped on your number one or number two Value but because you didn't know what it was, you simply got upset without really knowing why. When you know what your Values are, you get some warning!

When I first did this exercise, I discovered that my number one Value was respect. That was a surprise. I might have expected it to be in the top ten, but not necessarily number one. But then when I thought about it a bit more, it made sense; not only in the present, but that Value had also guided me in the past, too.

I spent my formative career years working in international marketing for large multinational corporations. I never really felt at home in that environment. I was not prepared to play office politics and my career suffered as a result. But the real reason I had to leave that environment was the complete lack of respect for me as an individual, or anybody else for that matter. As an individual, I didn't matter to the company. The only consideration was what the company could get out of me in my work.

Employees are a company's most important asset. Only recently is that being recognised in the business world with Employee Engagement being the latest buzzword. A company can have the most innovative product and the most sophisticated systems, but if employees are not cared for and motivated, the company's growth will be limited.

Now, as a behavioural therapist, it is essential that I respect my clients. I can't help them if I judge them, and that means I have to respect them, no matter what mess their lives might be in. If I judge them, then I am using my Map of the World which won't work for them because it's my Map. In order to help them I need to respect them and allow them to find their own Map. Being nonjudgemental was my number two Value.

Interestingly, in the process of writing this book my Values have changed significantly again. I have become much more aware of the need for cooperation and freedom. My top four Values are currently: **Connection, Freedom, Joy and Vitality**. As significant experiences happen to us (for example, becoming a parent for the first time) and as we gain more Self Awareness, our Values tend to change and deepen.

Most people have two to three Values Clusters which makes it easier to remember what our Values are on a day to day basis. In other words, the Values seem to fall into two or three groups in which they 'feel' the same, so that one of the words epitomises the other Values. Here are the top ten Values of a recent client:

- Strength

- Conscientiousness

- Love

- Community

- Independence

- Freedom

- Excitement

- Spontaneity

- Outgoingness

- Being supportive.

These words fall nicely into the following clusters:

- The <u>friendship</u> cluster: love, community, being supportive, outgoingness

- The <u>activity</u> cluster: freedom, excitement, spontaneity

- The <u>power</u> cluster: strength, conscientiousness, independence.

You may well find other words – or other Clusters – that suit your Map better, and that's great.

Knowing your Values consciously can change your life! To illustrate this outrageous claim, let me give you a couple of examples of past clients.

 Peter's Story:

Peter came to see me about four years ago with depression. He worked in one of the big City accountancy practices and was often in the financial pages of the newspaper. To his surprise his number one Value turned out to be Justice. When you think of it, how much justice is there involved in being an accountant? Worse than that, because he worked in the City, where, in his words, "dodgy deals were rife", he scored that Value -3 out of 10 at work in the Values exercise.

Not only was there no justice, but it was an environment he was increasingly unable to work in because of the injustice. The only way he had been able to find any evidence of justice at home was dishing it out to his children, but they'd grown up and left home years before. So, his score for justice at home was 0 out of 10. In other words, there was no justice in his life.

You might not think that's a big deal, but scores that low always foretell big changes afoot, if the person is going to turn their life around. Six months after seeing me, I received a postcard from him from Afghanistan. He'd been living in a tent and had never been so happy in his life. He was working for Amnesty International, and was honouring his number one Value every second of his waking day.

Assuming he came back to the UK, do you think he would go back into the City? Pretty unlikely I would say. I can tell you he hasn't been in the financial pages of the newspapers for well over three years. That one piece of information changed his life!

📖 Sarah's Story:

Sarah came to see me about twelve months ago, again with depression. When she did the Values exercise, she worked out that her number one and number two Values were Freedom and Excitement, and promptly burst into tears. When I asked why, she explained that when she had first started work, she'd typically come home on a Friday night and, on the spur of the moment, pack a backpack with jeans, Tee shirts and trainers and drive up to the Lake District for the weekend. However, she hadn't done that for well over a year.

When I asked why not, she took me through a typical week in her current life. She would be in the office most mornings before 8.00 a.m. and rarely got away before 7.30 p.m. at night. She'd arrive home exhausted, shove something in the microwave, pour herself half a bottle of wine and then go to bed. She did this five days a week and even went back into the office every Saturday morning. So where was the freedom? Where was the excitement? Clearly, there wasn't any.

She then said how embarrassed she was, because the answer for her depression was so obvious, but because, in her words, she'd been "like a rabbit in the headlights" and didn't know why her job was wrong, she was frozen and had done nothing about it. When she realised the impact of the wrong job on her freedom and excitement, she knew what to do. I got an excited email from her about six months ago. She'd got a new job, and had completely sorted out her work-life balance.

Unconsciously, both Peter and Sarah knew their working environments were wrong, but because they couldn't consciously see the impact of not honouring their Values, they were not taking action. As soon as their Values were out in the open, in consciousness, they could take action. Sometimes finding out what your Vales are, simply confirms that what you're doing is right.

📖 Ted's Story:

Ted's experience of finding his Values simply confirmed to him the reasons why he loved his work and why he'd had considerable success.

Ted has built up a very successful engineering business over twenty years and as he described his views on running a business to me, he was simply unconsciously outlining his Values. When he came to do the Values exercise, I was not at all surprised by the results.

He was telling me of a trip he had to make the following week. A chap at one of his branches who had been with the company for many years had an altercation with his new manager. Whilst Ted supported the manager, he planned to make the full day trip to make sure that his long-term employee was happy with the outcome of the discussions. Ted has a team of capable directors helping him run the business, but this was still a lot of time as the M.D. to devote to one employee... but not if your Values are things like loyalty, trust, "family". No wonder Ted had built a successful business with employee engagement initiatives like that!

Knowing what the Values in your unconscious filtering system are is crucial to having a measure of control in your life. If you are not honouring your Values, you're not going to be happy. It's as simple as that!

Chapter 5:
Left or Right?

> *"Your visions will become clear only when you can look into your own heart. Who looks outside, dreams. Who looks inside, awakens."*
>
> **Carl Jung**

What is Brain Dominance?

Brain Dominance is the way in which our preferred way of thinking and our personality is influenced by the way our physical brain is set up.

Most people have a physically dominant side that becomes most obvious when playing sport. We can be right or left handed and right or left footed. It also of course shows up in writing or holding a knife and fork. Very few people are genuinely ambidextrous.

In fact, although it is much less obvious, we have a dominant eye as well.

 Instant Exercise:

Find a small object to look at ten to fifteen feet away from you and then hold up your hands, one behind the other, about ten inches away from your face and form the thumb and forefinger of each hand into a single circle. With both eyes open, get your chosen object into the middle of the circle, then close your right eye, open it again and then close your left eye. When you closed one of your eyes, the object will have disappeared from the circle, that's your non dominant eye.

Well, your brain has a dominant side too, which may come as a surprise, as we only have one brain. We have 2 arms, legs and eyes, so it's easy to spot the dominance. Brain Dominance is slightly more complex, but has far greater impact on the way we live our lives, and it is a major part of the unconscious filtering process.

The left side of your brain is the logical side that focuses on detail (numbers, science, language) and the right hand side of your brain is more creative and sees the big picture.

In addition, according to research carried out by Paul Maclean M.D., [1] the human brain has three levels, each with a different size, chemistry and function that reflects our development in evolutionary terms. Maclean's research suggests that each level has its own intelligence, memory and sense of space and time, and that they connect together to form one 'super brain'! He called the three brains - the reptilian brain, the mammalian brain and the neocortex or cerebral cortex.

The hierarchical order and indeed physical positioning within our skulls, tells us important information about how we evolved and how our brain functions. The reptilian brain arrived first and is the most primitive area. It is located where the spinal cord meets the brain and is responsible for coordination and movement. It supports the basic life functions including breathing, heart rate, and levels of wakefulness and sleep.

Scientists believe that the cerebellum, part of the reptilian brain, is where simple learned programmes around movement (e.g. riding a bike) are stored. There's almost no conscious thought required to ride a bike! But other programmes memorised and activated by the cerebellum include emotional reactions, habits, conditioned behaviours and unconscious reflexes.

The mammalian brain arrived next and is literally wrapped round the reptilian brain. It is the part of the brain that looks after our unconscious autonomic nervous system. The mammalian brain is responsible for emotions, because it controls the chemical balances within our body by automatically regulating body temperature, blood sugar, digestion and hormone levels. It is also responsible for the fight or flight response, which is the state we go into the instant we recognise danger. We will be discussing it in greater detail in Chapter 9.

Finally, the neocortex is formed over the top of the mammalian brain and is the grey, bulbous mass that most of us think is our total brain. The neocortex is where our capacity to learn, reason and think is kept, as well as our free will, which is what really distinguishes us from other animals.

Although the brain appears as a single grey mass, it is made up of lots of different parts and as we grow up we begin to use different parts of our brains more than others. There has been a large amount of debate over which has the greater influence over our development as children, nature or nurture.

In fact the answer is both. Our brain starts developing in the womb on the forty second day, when the first neuron develops. By the time we are sixteen our physical brain and, indeed a large part of our personality, are well formed.

However, the brain has the ability to reorganise itself as a result of life experiences; this is called brain plasticity. So the way the brain is 'wired' is constantly changing and this is why we **can** make massive changes in our lives.

Thinking Preferences and the Different Parts of the Brain

The human brain is of course extremely complex, but in a simplified model we can associate four different parts of the physical brain with different styles of thinking. The left side of the brain is associated with logical, rational, analytical and sequential thinking and tends to focus on detail by breaking everything down into different elements. The right side of the brain is intuitive, emotional and expressive and looks at the bigger picture searching for connections and similarities.

The upper part of the brain is about reasoning and thinking - this is the cerebral part of the brain. The lower part of the brain is about emotion, humour and memory - this is the limbic part of the brain. A simplified Brain Dominance model is therefore made up of 4 quadrants:

Upper left brain: this quadrant focuses on 'logical' thinking, so people who are dominant here tend to like neatness and precision. They are good with detail and think sequentially. They are good at planning, tend to be cautious and are not great risk takers.

Lower left brain: the left brain hemisphere is associated with specific reasoned thinking. People with a strong dominance here tend to be good with numbers and words, are good at analysing things, breaking things down and they like to know how everything works.

Upper right brain: this part of the brain is for 'blue sky thinking', looking at the bigger picture. People dominant in this quadrant often question the 'rules'; they are excited by new things and are happy to take risks.

Lower right brain: this part of the brain focuses on 'emotional' thinking. People dominant here tend to be good listeners and empathetic. They are good at recognising nonverbal communication (body language, tonality). They are 'people' people and are interested mainly in the human aspects of any situation.

Most people are dominant in two quadrants, having a preference for two thinking styles. You may even recognise some of the characteristics in yourself. It is important to note that brain dominance is only showing a preference, it is not about somebody's abilities. If someone is primarily left brained, it doesn't mean they don't like people! If someone is right brained, it doesn't mean they hate numbers! Similarly, if someone is right handed, it doesn't mean they can't catch a ball with their left hand. Unconsciously they will just put their right hand out to catch it.

Why is it useful to understand our Brain Profile?

Just as we tend to have a preference for catching a ball with one hand rather than the other, we will also have preferences for which parts of our brain we prefer to use for processing the two million bits of information that bombard us every second. Since the various parts of the brain process information in different ways, a person's brain dominance strongly influences how they think, who they are and the way they behave. A person's Brain Dominance therefore forms the foundation of their personality.

Learning about your own Brain Dominance can therefore benefit you in all sorts of ways:

Strengths and weaknesses: we can understand why we are good at some things but not so good at others. Why we are more motivated to get involved in certain tasks and ignore other activities. Knowing our brain dominance helps us to play to our strengths.

Self confidence: we tend to lack confidence when we struggle to do something or find that others are much better than we are. Brain Dominance simply means that we all have different strengths and weaknesses and that we can all excel in different ways. When you know your own brain dominance profile, you can be more confident in playing to your strengths, more accepting of your own weaknesses, as well as those of other people. It enables us to feel better about ourselves.

Communication and relationships: because we are all different, an understanding of brain dominance can improve our communication and so our relationships with other people. So for example, if you prefer lots of data and facts, and I just want the 'big picture', we need to be approached very differently. Understanding these differences and learning how to recognise them, enables us to tailor our approach accordingly.

Career and Work Life Balance: a lot of people make career decisions based mainly on financial factors like pay and package, but research suggests that successful people succeed because they tend to be in jobs that they are suited to and enjoy. By understanding your brain dominance profile you are better able to match your career choices to your thinking preferences and even your personality, and so reduce stress and improve your performance.

Daniel Pink [2] puts brain dominance into a critically important context for the future. He argues that left brain dominance has brought us more wealth than our grandparents could ever have dreamed of. But this wealth has had a rather ironic effect, in that the very dominance of left brain thinking has now lessened its own significance. The world is about to change dramatically. There are three main drivers behind this change.

The left brain derived prosperity has now placed a premium on more right brained concerns like beauty, spirituality and emotion. It's not good enough to produce a cheap, efficient product anymore, it needs to be beautiful and unique as well.

Western business has already begun a huge shift in activity. The left brain derived increases in efficiency brought about by computers are now nothing special and IT jobs are flowing at an alarming rate to low cost centres like China, India and the Philippines. Outsourcing is a huge industry and it doesn't contribute much to the coffers of the United States or Europe! There's no great requirement for left brained computer programmers in the West anymore. These jobs are carried out just as efficiently, but at a distinctly cheaper rate elsewhere.

When society depended on mass production, right brain thinking was almost irrelevant. Then as we moved into the knowledge based economy, typified by the internet explosion, right brained thinking was recognised but still secondary to left brained thinking. Now as the Western world evolves again, right brained thinking is becoming the most valued. All this in thirty years! Unfortunately very little of this knowledge has found its way into one area where it really matters: education.

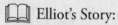 ## Elliot's Story:

Elliot came to see me with a complete lack of motivation at school. At primary school he had been quite good at all subjects, although he'd enjoyed English, drama, music and art the most.

He'd done OK in his first year and a half at secondary school but as the pace was hotting up with GCSE's on the horizon, Elliot's Mum was getting more and more concerned. Not only were his grades falling dramatically in Science and Maths, but he'd fallen out with his English teacher and his grades were even dropping in his favourite subjects.

It turned out that Elliot's father was an engineer and his older sister was reading medicine at university. The family put little value on the arts and so, given that this was where Elliot's strengths lay, he felt that whatever he did was not good enough. Excelling in English, Drama and Music was not good enough.

Indeed, the whole educational system is biased towards Maths and Sciences.

When I explained the concept of Left Brain Right Brain to Elliot and expanded on what Daniel Pink said, as mentioned above, Elliot's motivation and pride in his work soon came back. He has now faced up to his father and made it clear how he feels about what direction his future education will take. He has become a champion for the Drama department at school. And needless to say, all of his grades have gone back up, but particularly those of his favourite subjects.

The theme of brain dominance in schools is taken up by Sir Ken Robinson at the 2006 TED conference with a presentation called "Schools kill creativity". The web address is included in the Resources Section; I thoroughly recommend watching the video.

You can see how easily the Brain Dominance filter influences our own individual perceived reality. If this is of further interest to you, **My Brain Limited** offers an excellent online profiling system, which is simple and quick to use and will help you understand your own preferred thinking style. Please see the listing in the Resources Section.

Chapter 6:
Kids Matter!

> *"Everything depends on upbringing."*
>
> **Leo Tolstoy**

The Mind Matrix ©

The next filter for the two million bits of information hitting our system every second is our Childhood Programming.

The nature versus nurture debate is widely known, but our particular personality is not conditioned 100% by either, it has to be a mixture of both. Our genetic inheritance includes long term conditioning on how to survive and adapt, built up over hundreds of generations, but our short term conditioning, going back perhaps just two generations, gives us our individuality. This becomes the 'nature' of who we are. In addition, we take in information from interacting with our environment, particularly in the early years of our development. This becomes the influence of 'nurture', as we make more connections from our experiences of learning both formally and informally. [1]

However, environmental circumstances (nurture) can change what would have been our genetic destiny. If our parents are both hugely intelligent academics, but we are malnourished in the first two years of our development, the likelihood of our following our parents into the 'ivory towers' of academia is significantly reduced, as nutrition helps to dictate how the brain develops. Joseph Ledoux[2] states that inherited genetic programming only accounts for 50% of our personality traits. We only inherit our parents' knowledge and emotional patterns as the platform for who we become.

Every time we learn or experience something new, we change the neural connections in our brains and the potential for who we are. So nature kindly gifts us with some necessary built in programming when we are born, but it is then up to us to build our own neural patterns and connections.

An American study showed that 96% of four year olds had good Self Esteem and a good sense of self. They believed they could be anything they wanted to be: astronauts, pilots, cowboys. Scarily, the study showed that by the time these kids were 18 less than 5% had good Self Esteem or sense of self.

As we grow older, our Self Esteem is knocked by external influences: a teacher telling us we can't do a maths sum, parents telling us we're clumsy, friends telling us we can't cook. We take these messages on board and they become part of our Self Image. We then look for evidence to support the poor self image. We mess a recipe up and then say to ourselves: "well I always knew I couldn't cook" and then give up. A baby doesn't give up trying to walk because he falls over for the tenth time. He knows he's going to walk! [3]

Again, in the interests of keeping the model simple, I am not going to descend into the realms of deep Freudian psychology. It is completely unnecessary to go into great detail to understand what our Mind is doing. I break childhood down into four sections, during each of which the Mind is learning in very different ways and influenced by very different sources of 'wisdom'. The first part is in the womb, before birth, the second is roughly birth to seven years old, the third is roughly seven to twelve years old, and the final part is the teenage years.

In Utero Programming

It is common knowledge that cigarette and alcohol intake by the mother during pregnancy can lead to quite drastic postnatal effects on the child. Foetal alcohol syndrome impairs brain development of the unborn child, whilst nicotine and carbon monoxide intake from smoking cigarettes contributes to stillbirth, premature birth and low birth weight. Women are also generally speaking aware that they should take care of their nutritional intake to maximise the health of their baby.

However, consideration is rarely given to the mother's mental state during pregnancy. We will be discussing the effects of the 'fight or flight response' on us as adults in more detail in Chapter 9. Suffice it to say for now, that when we are anxious or fearful, the body will secrete higher levels of adrenalin, cortisol and noradrenalin to keep us alert and the body effectively goes into shock when we perceive that our life is in danger. The perceived danger can be physical (being beaten up) or these days financial (worries about paying bills). The hormones cortisol, adrenalin and noradrenalin are in fact poisonous in excess levels and are often experienced in extended stress or anxiety.

Since the foetus is dependent on its mother for nourishment of all kinds, the chemical balances of the mother's body will of course be 'fed' into the foetus. There have been numerous scientific studies showing the connection between emotional and behavioural disturbances in a child as it grows up and the stress of the mother during pregnancy. These include Learning Difficulties, ADHD (Attention Deficit and Hyperactivity Disorder) (Linnet et al. 2003; Laucht et al. 2000), aggression and disruptive behaviour, and temperamental difficulties (O'Connor 2002).

This underlines the seriousness of domestic violence, which accounts for between 20% and 33% of A&E visits by women in the USA. [4] Not only is the mother at risk physically, but so is a foetus in pregnancy due to excess levels of adrenalin and cortisol.

A mother holding down a job right the way through pregnancy might be admirable in many ways, but if it comes at the cost of extreme stress, it's a cost the baby has to pay as well as the mother. So the emotional state of the parents, particularly the mother, can have a huge effect on the way a child and particularly its brain develops.

Imprint Period (0-7 years)

From nought to seven years old we do not have a Conscious Mind, as such. We haven't developed what's called the Critical Faculty, the ability to decide what's good and what's bad. Little children are like sponges! Because there's no Conscious Mind trying to analyse incoming information, the child just sucks the information in.

The brain operates at different wavelengths, each of which produce a different effect upon the body and the Mind. Low frequency delta waves are associated with a state of extreme relaxation, whilst high frequency beta waves are associated with normal alert activity and behaviour. Interestingly brainwave activity has a profound effect on how young children learn. Dr Rima Laibow describes how, between birth and two years old, human brain activity operates mainly at delta waves. Between two and six the child's brainwave activity gets more active and falls into the theta range.[5]

This is because the child doesn't develop the critical faculty (i.e. Conscious Mind) until after the age of six. This is why children can 'download' such a huge amount of information. They aren't rationalising or analysing, something most adults are pretty good at!

Hypnotherapists take their clients into delta and theta states because they are much more suggestible and programmable states of mind. Because toddlers are constantly in delta and theta, their minds are always open to programming. They are vulnerable and there's an argument for parents to have basic hypnotherapy training to ensure that all the messages are healthy!

Now, there's a good side to this and a bad side! The good side is that this is why a child can be trilingual by the age of three. How do they do that?! The rest of us go to school at the age of ten and start to learn French, and it's already a whole different ball game. This is why professional sports teams are taking interest in younger and younger children. The earlier they can begin building their skills, the better their performance will be in the long run. Between birth and six years old, the child can undertake his learning without the need to analyse everything.

However, since the child doesn't have the ability to decide what's right or wrong, he takes in the bad information too. Child abuse has a massive effect on the emotional stability of the child, and of course the future adult. Most child abuse happens before the age of six and is carried out within the family. The child has no real way of knowing that the experience is 'wrong' and on a conscious level takes it as a 'normal' part of growing up.

It is only when the child compares his experiences with peers at school that he realises the abuse is not 'normal'. The child then feels extreme shame and guilt, assuming that the experience was his own fault. In reality, how can it be their fault? They were a small child and the perpetrator was an adult. A significant proportion of my clients over the last ten years were abused as children and one of the most difficult areas for them to deal with is the shame and the guilt. Many of them refer to themselves as 'rotten to the core' and they all use the same expression.

If a child has been abused by his parent, how is he supposed to develop any sense of Self Esteem or Self Love? What is worse, that person as an adult, has the incoming two million bits of information every second going through the abusive experience as well as any emotional programming (we will visit this in more detail in Chapter 9) taken on board as a result. So between nought and seven we are extremely vulnerable in terms of how our emotional maturity develops into adulthood.

My own babyhood experience of severe asthma and regular panic visits to hospital (my survival was only rated at 50/50 for many months) must have led to programming that I wasn't good enough. My parents couldn't be there the whole time (in fact in those days parents weren't allowed to stay overnight) and the nurses couldn't possibly have given me the same level of attention as my parents would have. As a result, I have suffered from very low Self Esteem for most of my life.

The positive outcome was that I learnt to become very self sufficient. In fact, it's probably that part of the programming that enabled me to survive, tipping the 50/50 odds the right way! Unfortunately, this also led to an inability to ask for help. All this programmed in before I was seven!

Interestingly, now that I understand all of this (what was unconscious has been brought into Consciousness), the programming has all changed. I now feel good about myself. I have been able to develop a very healthy sense of Self Worth and I've even learned to ask for help!

So, how aware are you of what actually happened to you in your early childhood? How much have you unconsciously blocked out? How have those childhood experiences affected your personality and your beliefs as an adult? Exercises at the end of the chapter will help you think this through.

Modelling Period (8-12)

At about the age of eight, we fully develop the critical faculty and begin to work out what is right and wrong. It is also the period at which the child becomes much less self orientated; they start to realise that there's a whole big, wide world out there beyond themselves. They have to learn how to live in this new world as quickly as possible, so from whom are they going to learn? The adults, of course, who are doing this living 'stuff' every day. So between about eight and twelve we learn primarily from our parents, teachers, grandparents and any significant aunts and uncles, those are the people we look up to.

Whilst much of our behaviour is unconsciously programmed by our parents in this stage of childhood, it is likely that they also pass on some of their temperaments, personality traits and attitudes. We then take this on as our own genetic coding. The most commonly repeated behaviours will produce the most densely 'hardwired' neural patterns. We can literally inherit similar thoughts, behaviours and emotional states.

However, this only gives us the genetic propensity to follow our parents in their emotional tendencies. For example, depression or victimhood may develop and on a more positive note, the predisposition to practise a musical instrument or sporting skills.[6]

It always amazes me that some of my clients, as children, seem to have gone out of their way not to copy their parents. So, for example, they became extremely diligent and action orientated when one of their parents was lazy. However, the norm does seem to be that we take on similar emotional tendencies to our parents. The important thing is though, that we're not necessarily stuck with those traits if they are negative.

Interestingly, we can take on all sorts of programming that's not naturally ours, because the process is completely unconscious. A lot of programming around food starts here. The child can start to copy mum (or dad) in worrying about the size of his thighs or tummy. He can start worrying about food intake because mum's on a diet, or even start comfort eating, if that's what mum and dad are doing.

The roots of full blown eating disorders often start here. I see clients for weight loss and it is common for a client to sit down and immediately start talking about problematic genes: "We're all fat in our family, it runs in the family... my mum's fat, my dad's fat, my brother's fat, my grandmother's fat," etc. etc....! Very few people are genetically predisposed to be fat. It's in the programming!

Another example of Childhood Programming during this period is fears and phobias. When I first began practising as a therapist, it used to amaze me how many of my clients had fears or phobias that ran in families, particularly spiders and mice, but also more invasive phobias like claustrophobia. After a few times of tracking back with the client to find out where their fear of spiders came from, and coming across a memory of them standing on the sofa next to mum who was screaming at somebody to get the spider out of the room, it all fell into place!

This is also a very important period for the child in its parental relationships. The modern preoccupation with success and earning money, means many parents unwittingly start putting huge pressure on their kids at this age to 'achieve'. This can lead to 'perfectionism', which is lethal, as perfection does not exist, it's a concept. But as soon as the child reaches what it thought perfection was, the goalposts move!

Excess parental pressure to achieve at this age can set the child up for failure. If the child keeps setting his targets too high and failing, feelings of failure and lack of Self Esteem aren't far behind. This is absolutely not to say that encouraging a child to do his best is a bad thing. It is the difference between achieving 100% and 102%. The latter's not possible! The child can very quickly set up the internal programme of expecting to fail to reach the target, when failure means anything less than 100%.

The counter example of this is just as bad, where the parents have no real emotional connection with the child.

How's the child supposed to develop Self Esteem, when the parents aren't interested in looking at the latest paint splodges representing the family home? Some of my adult clients with low Self Esteem hadn't even realised that they had a distant relationship with their parents:"It's just how things were". This sort of parental relationship sets up a permanent feeling of neediness and worthlessness as well as the need to be constantly recognised. They spend their childhood (and indeed their adult life) trying to please and craving recognition from their parents.

Many people assume that they have had happy childhoods, until they start to 'unpack' them a bit. It's not to say that they had an awful time growing up, it's just not perhaps as rose tinted as they thought.

📖 Henry's Story:

Henry had a huge issue with abandonment, which was now affecting his marriage so badly that his wife was starting to consider the very thing he feared most. When we looked at his Childhood Programming, he was sent to boarding school at the age of seven and was badly bullied in his first two years. He wasn't actually abandoned, his parents merely lived abroad. His first Christmas home from boarding school he got mumps and had to be quarantined on Christmas Eve. It was pretty bad luck but again he wasn't actually abandoned. However, you can see how the emotional trauma of abandonment would start to build up in his unconscious programming.

Does any of this ring a bell for you?

Socialisation Period (Teens)

Once the child reaches his or her teens, the parents and the family start to take a back seat in terms of influence and peers become more important. The teenage years are generally misunderstood and actually incredibly important in terms of emotional development. We've just spent five years learning from our parents: "Well now it's my turn to decide what's right or wrong, not my parents or my teachers. It's all about what I think!"

So in order to learn for themselves what is acceptable and what's not, teenagers inevitably end up pushing the boundaries and most of us learn best by making mistakes. Sound familiar? The difficulty comes in the very different locations of the boundaries of acceptability between the parents and the teenagers. In fact, that's exactly where the arguments come in.

I am often asked when reaching this part of The Mind Matrix © model in a workshop: "OK Mark, how do I bring my teenagers up?"? I can't say this is my area of expertise, particularly as my own girls have been angels in their teens, so I can't even answer from personal experience.

However, because of my experience with thousands of clients and understanding of how the Mind works, I am convinced of one thing about the teenage years - if you keep your kids under your thumb, they are either going to grow up into timid adults and struggle to reach their full potential and happiness, or they're going to rebel! And in many ways the quicker they rebel, the better. It's rather messy when we rebel in our thirties or forties!

📖 John and Mary's Story:

Two people who lived next door to each other, came to see me as clients about four years ago. Mary came first for depression. I was running through this part of The Mind Matrix © and she suddenly said: "You must see my next door neighbour, John. He's incredibly stressed at work, but the real problem is that his teenage boys are going off the rails and he feels helpless in trying to do something about it."

John duly came to see me and when I reached this part of The Mind Matrix © model he burst into tears. He hadn't realised that he was following his father's relationship pattern with him as a teenager, with his own boys. His father was in the army and their whole household was completely 'regimented'. As a typical teenager, John rebelled and came home from boarding school one holiday with a mild 'Mohican', annoying his father. It was the early eighties during the punk era! John was having big problems with his sons because they were goths with dyed black hair and black make-up.

As soon as John understood the relevance of his own experience as a teenager with his dad, he knew what he had to do. His boys had spent years being almost perpetually 'grounded'. So he called them up to the breakfast table at the weekend, following our first appointment, and literally put his hand up to take responsibility for the combative relationship they had. He promised to back off and give them more space, which he duly did. The make-up went within four to six weeks and the dyed hair took a bit longer to grow out!

I received an email from Mary recently to tell me that one of her daughters was getting engaged to one of John's sons. She was delighted because both John's sons were now perfect son-in-law material! They were respectful, confident and communicated extremely well. She had forbidden her daughter from going out with either of them four years previously because she didn't trust them at all. She reckoned they were responsible for some fires in their village.

The lesson here is that teenagers are not kids, although they're not adults either! It's a fine line we tread as parents, but I believe most teenagers will respond to being treated as adults and being trusted. The teenage years are when we discover who we are, it's when we build our sense of Identity. We need the space to do that!

As a child, we receive huge amounts of praise and unconditional love. We're told how special we are, which reinforces our positive self image. But as we get older, these positive messages become fewer and fewer. What is more we learn to conform. As a teenager, we don't want to be different. But this is precisely the time we begin to form our sense of self – our identity – and as we grow older, we learn that it is safe to stay within that identity. We forget that we can change anytime we wish.

I see clients every week who, for whatever reason, didn't get their teenage years. People with eating disorders rarely have a sense of Identity, as they've spent these really important growth years isolated and internally focussed in an entirely different way. Other clients have had major illnesses like M.E. or recurring glandular fever and missed time at school. Others had problems making friends at school because their parents moved every two years.

📖 Linda's Story:

One recent client, Linda, was typical of many women I see in this respect. She came for depression, but when we 'unpacked' things, it became immediately clear that she had no sense of who she was and this was a large part of what was preventing her from moving on. She had been going out with the same boy from the age of thirteen until they got married and had kids.

They were so wrapped up in each other, that they didn't really have their teenage years of sharing the boundary pushing behaviour with their mates. Having married at 19 and a child following quickly thereafter, they had both had to grow up pretty quickly. However, as they grew up they grew apart, so much so that they ended up getting divorced. Linda coped with the divorce really well and was a marvellous example of a good one parent family.

When she reached her late thirties, however, her life collapsed when her kids left home. This was much more than 'empty nest syndrome'. Her whole life had been 'externally referenced'. She'd always seen herself as a girlfriend and then a wife and finally as a mum, and suddenly she was none of them.

She had her whole sense of self snatched away and found that all her relationships were falling apart as a result, even her work ones, which had nothing to do with her family. She no longer had a base from which to live in the world. So, our job was to help her discover who she was and to do that essential development work that she should have been able to do in her teens. It is extremely common for people with low Self Esteem to have had very 'quiet' teenage years.

Two years on she is married to a very different man, has a new job and is travelling a lot: something she'd always wanted to do, but never quite dared!

What were the experiences that moulded your development as a teenager?

The patterns and programmes we develop as children stay with us as deeply unconscious filters for how we live our lives as adults. Even though the programmes are no longer relevant, our Unconscious continues to play them regardless, until we change them. Simply understanding the unconscious programmes you developed as a child and bringing them into consciousness, will allow you to let go of the ones you don't need any more.

The last thing I want to say on Childhood Programming before I move on is:

**To be Authentic in the future,
you have to be Authentic about the past!**

Chapter 7:
Society Expects...

> *"Often people attempt to live their lives backwards; they try to have more things, or more money, in order to do more of what they want so that they will be happier. The way it actually works is the reverse. You must first be who you really are, then do what you really need to do, in order to have what you want."*
>
> **Margaret Young**

The Mind Matrix ©

The Mind Matrix ©

Values
Childhood Programming
Cultural Programming
Beliefs

2 Million bits of information per second

5-9 bits per second

Filtering

Autopilot

Mind chatter
What if?
R.A.S.

Reality

We are receiving so much more information from the world around us than our grandparents did (more in one day than they received in a year!). We are continually bombarded with messages by the media pushing us this way and that.

The focus on celebrities and reality TV has also done a huge amount of damage in terms of allowing us to be ourselves. There are ideals put in front of us every day about how we should be, how we should look and behave and so many people end up aspiring to an ideal they can never reach. This inevitably leads to a lack of Self Esteem, which in turn can lead to stress and depression.

Unfortunately, this continuous cultural pressure slides underneath our conscious awareness and alters our minute by minute filtering system, which in turn changes how we see the world and alters our reality, and takes us away from just being ourselves.

Education

There is massive unconscious pressure to conform to what society expects us to be all the way through school, into early adulthood and beyond. Seth Godin has a lovely expression for the conforming process we are put through as young people, 'sheepwalking'! He points out that teaching kids to conform is safer and easier than encouraging the students to be themselves, to develop their sense of individuality and then have to deal with the anticipated chaos that the system expects to result. [1]

So the modern education process dulls our sense of self and forces us to conform and we then end up doing that in all areas of our life. What this educational strategy misses is the fact that happy, motivated students learn better and faster. What is more, the creativity brought about by kids thinking differently and motivated to learn, will multiply that learning exponentially.

Even universities are churning out reasonably well educated sheep, that is, people who are compliant and who conform. That's not what is needed in a world that is changing so quickly every day. We need people who think outside of the box more than ever. What is worse, companies often go out of their way to employ compliant employees who they then govern with fear: "follow the rules or you'll get fired"!

We need to stop 'sheepwalking' and follow our own rules. This doesn't mean going out of our way to be difficult or upset the apple cart. It just means finding our own path and following it regardless of what others think.

Today, society's most powerful source of conformity is the drive for money and success. We are brought up to believe that we are only successful if we earn loads of money! However, as we all intuitively know, lots of money doesn't automatically make us happy. Surely happiness is a better measure of success? Ask any parent what they really want for their kids and they will say they just want them to be happy. As parents, however, most of us follow the cultural conditioning that happiness means they have to earn lots of money!

Success

Ever since the end of the Second World War, society has told us that we must be 'the best that we can be'. That is what will make us happy. Success in our life becomes the hidden byword for living. Parents have been pushing children to improve themselves for generations. However, in today's society we've taken it to another level: pushy parents are a media phenomenon. It is now ingrained in us almost from birth that we have to continually strive to do our best and the expectations are getting higher and higher and for most people, further and further from possibility.

This has led to a common problem amongst many of my clients, which is a combination of 'perfectionism' and low

Self Esteem, which shows up most dramatically in eating disorders. It is a lethal cocktail of emotions. Perfectionism means setting oneself unrealistically high goals, which, when one fails to reach them, inevitably means beating oneself up for being 'so useless'.

The problem here is the way society measures success. Surely one of the greatest successes is being a happy family and bringing your kids up to be confident, rounded individuals, happy to be who they are? But motherhood, despite the influences of feminism, is still a lowly 'profession'. Surely being a good mum or dad is the most important job in the world? You don't need 'loadsa money' to be a good parent, indeed the hours required for both parents to have so-called successful careers, militates against being a good parent.

Sally's Story:

In fact Sally's story is the perfect example of this. She came to see me for a lack of confidence and stress; it transpired that she felt she'd never lived up to her father's expectations despite running a successful hairdressing business with six very active "chairs"!

She was constantly pressurising herself to grow the business and with a major decision imminent her stress was ballooning. She was about to double the size of the shop and go into beauty treatments as well.

She readily identified with the lethal emotional cocktail of low self esteem and perfectionism. When we looked at what was important in her life, it was simple: family. Part of her feeling of failure was not

> being a good enough Mum to her daughter, because she felt she wasn't "there" for her enough.
>
> As a family they were "comfortably off", so she decided to turn their family life on its head. Instead of expanding the business, she sold it. She now has another daughter and as a full-time Mum feels really good about herself and her family.

Money

Success in the 20th and 21st centuries has been all about money. That's how we measure success. The more you've got, the more successful you are. Interestingly, the more you've got doesn't mean the happier you are. The cover notes on Oliver James's splendid book *Affluenza* states the position perfectly:

> "An epidemic of *Affluenza* is sweeping the English-speaking world, an obsessive, envious, keeping-up-with-the-Joneses, that makes us twice as prone to depression, anxiety and addictions than people in other developed nations. And now we are infecting the rest of the world with this virulent virus." [2]

He outlines how the culture of English-speaking nations has been hijacked by what he calls the *Affluenza* virus, which he defines as: "the placing of a high value on money, possessions, appearances (physical and social) and fame". These values have been around for centuries, but what is different since the seventies is that they are not just those of the upper echelons of society, but of almost everybody.

Part of the cause of this is the power of advertising. People don't buy on the basis of needs any more, but on the basis of wants. So soap's not about being clean, it's about being beautiful. Cars aren't about getting from A to B, they're about status. Contemporary advertising makes us feel inadequate if we don't have product X. What is worse, it subtly promises something that the product cannot possibly provide. Using a certain make-up brand isn't going to make you into Kate Moss!

The other great contributor to this shift in values is the dominance of American TV and films, with their fabulously wealthy and beautiful characters (remember shows like *Dallas* and *Dynasty*?). These programmes portray what is seen as normal and are then backed up by the TV ads that come around every twenty minutes. It's not about keeping up with the Joneses next door anymore, but with the celebrities we see on TV. The bar has been raised and the vast majority of us will find ourselves wanting in this comparison and beat ourselves up as a result.

In the fifties, celebrities were untouchable. Average people wouldn't have dreamt of comparing their lives with Elvis or Marilyn Monroe. TV shows like *Big Brother* have made it seem that celebrity status is within relatively easy reach. When asked what they want to be when they grow up, kids will now often respond, 'a celebrity' as though it were a profession!

The position for women is much worse than for men. Their education and income have increased at a dramatically higher rate than they have for men since 1950, but a young woman today is also three times more likely to be depressed than in 1950 and twice as likely to suffer from depression as a man. This is partly due to the fact that the status of being a mother has plummeted. No sense of self esteem is attached to possibly the most important 'job' in the world.

What is worse, the materialistic lifestyle pushes people into taking on a huge mortgage in order to buy the big house to impress others and makes the dual income household a necessity. The woman can't afford to be at home for long.

In southern Mediterranean countries (and even in Britain before the Industrial Revolution) people live in extended families, where there are always relatives on hand to help with the kids! So many women in Anglo Saxon countries now have to go back to work just when their children need the close relationship most.

It has been proved in many studies, that lack of care by the mother between the ages of six months and three years creates a fear in the child that the carer is not emotionally available, an anxiety which carries through into adulthood.

Our modern obsession with 'things' or 'stuff' confuses having with being. As Eckart Tolle says: "For modern man, it's not really "I think, therefore I am" as Descartes suggested, but "I have, therefore I am" that dictates how we live." We think the more we 'have', the happier we'll be – and capitalism is built on that – and because we're trained to want more, for us as individuals it's an endless pursuit for happiness, and for economics it's an endless source of growth.[3]

Money does not make us happy and in many ways, it's not even what it buys us that makes us happy either. You only need to look at the terrible emotional state some lottery winners get into, some even becoming suicidal.

As toddlers we get toys and often 'fall in love' with a particular toy and will shout at peers and siblings to "get off my toy... it's mine... get off". The toy becomes so important to us, that it becomes an extension of our identity, who we are. If mummy or daddy takes it away from us because we've been naughty, there's hell to pay! Interestingly, the next week, we get a new toy and the old favourite gets discarded. And so it goes on.

Then as adults, the toys just get bigger - for the boys it's the bigger, shinier car, the bigger house, the bigger TV, the latest phone or Apple gadget. For the girls, it's this year's shoes, fashion and make-up. We're always aspiring to the better possessions and we're continually comparing ourselves with everyone we know - our friends, relatives and colleagues and even with those we don't know, like celebrities. The problem is that this is a race without a finishing line! We will never have enough!

The easy availability of credit since the 70's has fuelled the desire for 'stuff'. Credit cards take advantage of a dangerous flaw in the emotional part of our brain. We overvalue immediate gains (like a new pair of shoes or a nice cake) at the cost of future expenses or pain (like high interests or putting on weight).The emotional brain simply doesn't understand hard-nosed facts like interest rates or pounds and kilos. Because there's little resistance to the emotional impulsivity, we just swipe away! [4]

Under the banner of 'Will's Wisdom', Will Smith tells us on YouTube, (See Resources): "Too many people spend money they haven't earned, to buy things they don't want, to impress people they don't like!" *Affluenza* in a nutshell!

Now, here's why my little rant on materialism is relevant to The Mind Matrix © and to the book! There's a fundamental problem with this approach to life and it's at the root of *Affluenza*. If we are always waiting to get bigger and better possessions and are anticipating that our life will be better in the future when we get them, then by definition, we are not happy with our lives now.

And guess what? We can only be happy in the present! Most people are literally destined to be unhappy, because they're always living their lives in their heads waiting for the future to get better. You can't be happy in the future - it hasn't happened yet!

In order to feed this endless quest for 'stuff' and in order to be 'successful', we are now conditioned into working longer and longer hours. Especially when there's a recession and we're fearful of keeping our jobs, the lifeline that provides all the 'stuff'. The need to climb the materialistic ladder has simply become more compelling and the speed with which we're trying to climb the ladder is faster. We just can't get enough and we're in a constant battle to outdo our neighbours.

The clients who come for S.A.D. (stress, anxiety and depression) are often particularly prone to the *Affluenza* virus! Part of my job in helping them out of these emotional straitjackets is to help them see how they are creating their problems. The solution is to get them off the treadmill of working every hour God sends in order to be able to pay the bills at the end of the month. Sound familiar?

We don't have time to be happy! But most of us don't even know what makes us happy, because we don't know what our Values are. We're so busy chasing things to make our lives better in the future that we can't see why we're unhappy now. Get off the treadmill and all becomes clear. The real problem is that we are living life at such a speed that we don't have the time to relax. The human system is not built to operate at full speed all day long, we need to take time out to relax.

Fifty years ago, we used to relax automatically. Many people walked to work and most kids certainly walked to school.

We can't do that anymore. In a drive for efficiency, work locations and schools are larger and more geographically concentrated. My village had its own primary school until about twenty five years ago and despite the fact that there are now more kids in the village, they have to be driven every morning to about four different schools, mainly in their parents' cars, as there aren't any bus services, because they died out about twenty years ago too!

Because we're working longer hours, we have less relaxation time in the evening and tend to be so tired that we prop ourselves in front of the TV for a few hours before going to bed. Unfortunately, the brain wave activity used to watch TV doesn't allow us to genuinely relax even though we're sitting still, it actually interferes with the ability to fall asleep easily.

The inevitable consequence of living in the 21st century is anxiety and it's now so ubiquitous, it has a special name: General Anxiety Disorder or G.A.D.!

Identity

Because we're conditioned to maximise our success in a materialistic way, we are constantly worrying about how other people see us. Do we measure up? Are we good enough? This doesn't stop at what car we're driving, it even goes as deep as how we look. Are we wearing the right clothes? Does my bum look big in this?! Instead of living life as ourselves, we're all trying to change who we are in order to fit in with the ideals that society gives us.

And how much worse could this be than the 'need' to be a size 0? Even for those who are naturally slender, that's a dangerously low weight ideal. The vast majority of women pursuing this ideal are therefore destined for misery, because they simply don't have the body type that can match up, no matter how much they diet. The media pressure around body image is a major contributing factor to the increase in the incidence of eating disorders.

In fact, one of the most interesting social discussions currently is that of Body Confidence, that is being happy with our bodies the way they are. It takes awareness and even courage to turn our backs on the glittering ideals that walk the red carpets and accept that we're not going to measure up.

This is made even worse by the profligate use of 'airbrushing', which makes the final image even more unreachable, as the photographer alters the model's waist to shoulder ratio, banishes blemishes on her skin and even changes her bust size. What chance does the average sixteen year old stand when she's bombarded by messages telling her this is what she must look like?

 Natasha's Story:

Probably the most impactful client relationship I've had over the twelve years is seeing Natasha in 2008. Natasha had been a model some years before coming to see me and had succumbed to the usual "we need you to lose four more pounds" routine. When she arrived, by her own admission, she was in a desperate state: she had been severely bulimic for many years, vomiting anything up to eight times a day and was so insecure and depressed that some days she couldn't leave her flat. In fact, having had years of therapy, she came as a last resort!

The key insight for Natasha was that this was not who she was; being "a bulimic" was not her Identity - it was a behaviour she was carrying out. For her, this was the key to unlocking her unconscious programming.

In fact, as you can see on my home page (**www.winningminds.co.uk**), Natasha is an intelligent, striking and dynamic woman. She now runs a highly visible and successful national Body Confidence Campaign: Body Gossip (**www.bodygossip.org**). She's taking the power of her own experience into the world and helping youngsters buck the trend and start loving their bodies and thereby start to feel good about themselves.

Hope for the Future

There are signs that people are waking up to the cultural pressures that the average person is subjected to, particularly with regard to money. The current recession has allowed some people to re-evaluate their attitude towards money. Hence the outrage about the size of bankers' bonuses when they seemed to have caused the recession in the first place.

One day when I was writing, the main article in the business section of The *Daily Telegraph* highlights a further disgrace within the banking system: "Bankers to face grilling over Libor scandal." The manipulation of rates of interest is fraud, pure and simple. Somebody should be put in jail for this!

Unbelievably, the same page features a further disgrace driven by materialistic greed: "US fines Glaxo record $3bn for mispromoting drugs." Have these companies forgotten who they're working for? In fact they are putting their customers' financial stability and health at risk. As another example, UK politicians have also underlined the disdain with which most people view them, with the expenses scandal.

When even the most money motivated people get off their treadmill and have a look at their life, amazing changes can happen.

📖 Freddie's Story:

Freddie, who came to see me for depression, had recently been made redundant from the City and was almost suicidal at our first session. He arrived in his City uniform (pinstripe suit and 'loud' tie) even though he hadn't been at work for over four months. It turned out that his job was effectively his identity and so the uniform was the only bit that he could hang on to. However, once he'd understood The Mind Matrix ©, he was able to get off the treadmill and see that he didn't really even like his job with the early starts and late finishes and that he wasn't in disgrace at all. He is now on a fast track government training scheme to qualify as a teacher and assistant headmaster. He could see that this was far more 'him' and that he had felt pressured into the City by the desire to look successful. He sees his new profession as honouring his desire to give something back.

In addition, there have been two quiet but significant social revolutions starting in recent years in the UK. Firstly, there are now thousands of people on waiting lists for allotments, which until recently were seen as a quaint throwback to the post war years. Now they're as trendy as VW campervans! The Values expressed by having an allotment are many (nurturing, organic food, Self Sufficiency, being in nature and of course community with others), but they also represent an opportunity to turn our backs on the suffocating pace of modern life.

Similarly, the number of families going camping over this period has risen hugely. Until recently, camping was either a hippie occupation or for those who couldn't afford to do 'proper' holidays. Indeed, the English Tourist Board is terrified each year – when the 'barbecue sizzler summers' we are promised turn out to be not just a damp squib but a deluge – that they'll lose the opportunity of the increased number of families holidaying in the UK.

Interestingly, the outcome turns out to be somewhat different. The general feeling reported in the newspapers is that, despite the rain, families have such a good time simply 'being' with each other and participating in the simple pleasures, that this might be a more permanent increase despite the weather. In fact, the trend had already started in the summer of 2008, before the financial world was thrown into disarray.

It takes extreme events to wake us up out of our dream world to see that society and therefore culture needs to change, and although the revolution has been happening for some years at a very subtle level, it takes time before the changes become mainstream. The problem is that from an unconscious information processing point of view, we are badly served by our current Cultural Programming.

The frightening speed of change in modern life explains a large part of the huge increase in mental illness that is evident today. The latest statistics show that 50% of all people will suffer from mental illness at some point in their lives and up to 20% of the population is mentally ill at any one time. 20% of all children are said to be mentally disturbed. [5]

To overcome this state of affairs, we urgently need to understand the inner processes that allow psychologically healthy human beings to mature, and go to great pains to bring up our children accordingly. This will require a massive shift in thinking for the vast majority of people. Without it we are surely heading to a point where mental illness endangers the very fabric of society.

However, human beings are highly adaptive. After all, that's the hallmark of our success as a species. When things get bad enough, we change. But things have to get **really** bad and we have to be in a lot of pain before we change. Well things are **really** bad - the change has to come soon!

It's very much worth your while figuring out what pressures you feel society might be unconsciously putting you under, since this changes the reality you create for yourself. By bringing these unconscious pressures into consciousness, you will be able to work out why you are not as happy as you might be. It will help you begin to think through the changes you might want to make in your life.

Chapter 8:
Is this the Real Life?
Is this just *Fantasy?*

"Man is what he believes"

Anton Chekhov

The Mind Matrix ©

Values
Childhood Programming
Cultural Programming
Beliefs

2 Million bits of information per second

5-9 bits per second

Filtering

Autopilot

Mind chatter
What if?
R.A.S.

Reality

Thanks to Queen for the chapter heading taken from the brilliant track 'Bohemian Rhapsody'!

Beliefs are things we BELIEVE to be true, but in fact they're not, **but** because 'in our heads', they are true, for us they are true... even though they are not! This makes it very difficult for us to realise that our thought patterns are Beliefs and not real! All of us are running negative or Limiting Beliefs in our Minds every day.

Your comfort zone, whilst it may be comfortable, is actually a self imposed prison! It is made up of *musts, must nots, can'ts* and other Limiting Beliefs about what you can and can't do. Our Beliefs form images in our Unconscious Minds and those images then dictate our behaviour, which in turn just proves the Limiting Belief!

A classic example is imagining we're going to forget some of a presentation at work. Our Mind creates a picture of us standing there tongue tied and the picture causes us to feel fear and what happens? We forget a key part of our presentation and that just goes to prove the point:"I'm rubbish at presentations!"

If we then dwell on it and keep reminding ourselves that we can't present, those neural pathways become more and more powerful, creating what seems like reality. Nope, only a belief! We then stay inside our comfort zone. The only way to learn and to develop is to get out of our comfort zone. [1]

The most common example of a Limiting Belief and in fact one that, at a certain level of Mind, we know is not true, is a lack of Self Esteem. Many people are 'playing a tape in their heads' about how useless they are and that they should be better than this. Nobody is born 'useless'! There may well be plenty of things we're not good at, but that doesn't make us useless.

But if we're continually telling ourselves that we are useless, it actually becomes true. If we think we're useless, then we behave in a useless way and people will then react to us as though we are useless, and that simply confirms to us what we've been telling ourselves all along. We 'square the circle'! But it's not actually true, we just think it is! Lack of Self Esteem is a Limiting Belief. Unfortunately most Beliefs are hidden because they are unconscious, so the best way for me to describe what I mean is to give you some examples of past clients.

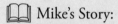 Mike's Story:

Mike, a multimillionaire, came to see me at the age of 52. He was born in the East End of London in abject poverty, one of nine children. So by anybody's standards, he had become an extremely successful man.

He came to see me for depression and as we were doing what I call the 'Self Discovery Process' part of our first session, something rather strange popped up out of the blue! He said to me: "Well I couldn't walk into town now, Mark and get myself a sandwich for lunch". "Why not"? I asked. "Well everybody looks at me". "How do you mean, everybody looks at you"? "Well I'm so ugly... look at me" and promptly burst into floods and floods of tears, calling himself Elephant Man and the ugliest man in the world!

Well, I must have been standing there with my mouth wide open! He wasn't ugly. He might not have been Brad Pitt or George Clooney, but he wasn't ugly, just an ordinary looking man. Then I made a connection to an observa-tion I had already made about him when I greeted him that, because I'm nonjudgemental, I'd simply let go. When he arrived he walked towards me and held out his hand, but he couldn't face me, his body was twisted away from me and there was absolutely no eye contact.

If he walked into town, completely avoiding eye contact, head down looking at the pavement and probably with a very awkward gait, people would certainly look at him. However, they'd look at him very briefly – probably with a sympathetic look – and carry on their way. The problem was that he would see this out of the corner of his eye and say to himself: "I know... I know I'm so ugly I shouldn't be allowed on the street". This simply confirmed his belief that he was ugly, he 'squared the circle'!

Imagine two million bits of information going through a filter that says he's the ugliest man on the planet. No wonder he was depressed, this Belief was devastating his life. He hadn't always suffered with this debilitating Belief. It would have been difficult to become a millionaire with that 'story' in his head! He had had a big shock in his life six months before coming to see me, when one of his companies had gone bust and whilst this hadn't threatened his home or his livelihood, it was devastating and he became depressed. In depression one's physical and mental coping mechanisms inevitably weaken and it's not un-common for Fears or Phobias to 'pop up out of the blue'!

When we carried on with the Self Discovery Process, we were having a look at his childhood and a picture came into his head. He was sitting in his pushchair as a toddler, with his dad bent over the pushchair, yelling at him in the middle of the High Street: "Stop your snivelling you ugly little brat." Not surprisingly, he burst into tears again.

Apparently he'd experienced a difficult birth and his head was quite badly squashed until the plates of the skull came together as a two to three year old. His dad had joked to his friends when Mike was first born about his "ugly little brat". However, as his marriage deteriorated and finally broke up, Mike's dad felt that Mike was responsible and made his life hell. The ugly little brat label became far more than a sinister joke. As Mike grew up and his dad disappeared from his life, the label disappeared too.

But as we've already discussed, childhood programming can lay dormant in the Unconscious until something triggers it. Losing his company and the consequent feelings of Self Loathing and Depression was clearly Mike's trigger. Once this conscious connection was made, helping Mike to shake off the debilitating belief that he was the ugliest man on the planet was relatively straightforward. A message repeated often enough can easily become a Limiting Belief in the Unconscious.

📖 Joanne's Story:

Another example of a devastating Limiting Belief was Joanne, who came for a fear of cold and lumpy food. Unbelievably (!), she worked in catering and came across cold and lumpy food every hour of the day, but things had got so bad, she'd decided to do something about it. As part of her homework, looking into Beliefs about her Fear, she burst into tears when she realised that at a very deep level, she'd spent the last 14 years of her life thinking she was insane. Thoughts about mental asylums and not letting people get close to her for fear of 'infecting' them pervaded her day.

> On completing the homework, she realised that of course she wasn't insane. She just had an unusual, unconscious Fear. However, with two million bits of information going through a filter that said she was insane, this would of course have a devastating effect on her life. Having made the connection, she rang me the following day to tell me that not only had her fear gone, but that for the first time at work she hadn't experienced any anxiety or sickness.

So many of us are running Beliefs that we have to be perfect, we have to work every hour God sends (remember Sarah from Chapter 4 on Values?), we're no good, we're this, we're that! Depression is a Belief. That is not to say that the person suffering isn't indeed suffering, but the problem is entirely in the head and the feelings of worthlessness, hopelessness and uselessness are Beliefs. Because the Beliefs are 'true' to us and are part of our filtering system, they have the ability to put a glass ceiling on our fun or our achievements and to completely wreck our lives and they're not even true!

Most beliefs are created from the previous filters in The Mind Matrix ©: our Values, our Brain Dominance, but principally our Childhood Programming and Cultural Programming.

Doctors, Negative Hypnosis and The Biology of Belief

Beliefs are often taken on board from comments made by people we revere and respect and become unconscious programming. Mike and his Dad are a good example. Other people in 'positions of authority' are doctors and teachers.

Hypnosis relies on a mutual sense of trust and respect between the client and the therapist. A good hypnotherapist is seen as being in a position of knowledge and authority. Incidentally, a common misconception is that the hypnotherapist has power over the client, but he/she doesn't. Even the best hypnotherapist in the world cannot make somebody do what they don't want to do!

However, you don't have to be a hypnotherapist to give a hypnotic suggestion, you just have to be in a respected position of authority. Mary came to see me recently for depression and had told her doctor that she was coming to see me. The last thing the doctor had said before she left his surgery was that "depression will always be in your life". Not surprisingly this had caused huge consternation for her every day for the two weeks before she came to see me.

This is a Belief passed on by many doctors. Anti-depressants, the medical profession's 'answer' to depression, are not actually a solution. Whilst they certainly help many people deal with their current bout of depression, they are only treating the symptoms. Until the cause is treated, of *course* depression can come back!

This is a classic piece of negative hypnosis, creating a Belief that she would always be depressed. Not true! Mary is no longer depressed. We have dealt with the things in her Mind that pulled her into depression. All she needs to do now is be wary when she gets into a low mood and let's face it, everybody has low moods! But with the hypnotic suggestion from her doctor, a low mood would mean her depression was coming back, making it a 'fait accompli'.

With total respect to GPs, who have an incredibly difficult and stressful job, they need to be very careful of their language when addressing patients, especially those in emotional states. I'm afraid that pretty much all of my depression clients arrive with the Belief that their depression will never go away completely.

They certainly need to deal with the causes of depression, to change their habitual thinking patterns and make lifestyle changes, but they don't need to permanently fear their depression returning. My job is to help them see that the depression is in their Mind and that, by making changes in their thinking patterns and lifestyle, not only can the depression go, but it can go permanently.

Similarly, anorexics and bulimics are told that they will always be in recovery. Not true! Again, they need to deal with the emotional reasons that caused them to begin the behaviour in the first place, and they need to change their thinking patterns and make lifestyle changes, but they don't have to have the spectre of what the medical profession calls their 'disease' hovering over their heads for the rest of their lives. This is a life sentence of misery that is absolutely not necessary.

Interestingly, the NHS treatment regime for anorexia confirms the Belief in the patient's Mind. They are made to write food diaries and keep to defined calorie controlled diets. The last thing an eating disordered person needs to think of is food, because food isn't the problem. It's simply become a habitual coping mechanism for emotional distress that probably started ten to fifteen years before.

The patient may put on weight when under the close scrutiny of the nurses, but as soon as they're released they go back to their old patterns. After all, they will always 'be in recovery'! Anorexia will always be in their lives! This isn't to say that they don't need to be aware that low feelings could potentially bring back their old patterns and that they need to change their behaviour but if they have the Belief that anorexia is always there, it pretty much guarantees the old patterns will come back. This Belief takes away any control that the patient might have had over their life.

The potential for negative hypnosis even applies to physical ailments. I appreciate that specialists have a legal responsibility to ensure that the patient is fully aware of the state of their health, but to tell someone that they have three months to live is literally a 'death sentence'. There's the doctor with his/her white coat and stethoscope round his/her neck, so of course the patient's going to believe them, and lo and behold the words become reality.

This exact scenario happened to the mother-in-law of somebody who used to work for me, despite the fact that the daughter-in-law had specifically asked to deliver that sort of news if the need arose. She understood the power of negative hypnosis. Unfortunately, the specialist delivered the 'death sentence' in her absence, thereby taking away any hope of recovery. My colleague's mother-in-law died two days after the three months were up! I am not asking doctors to give the patient a naive sense of false hope, but there is a way of delivering the news without guaranteeing a negative outcome, i.e. death!

The proof for the validity of this approach is laid out in one of the most revolutionary books of science: *The Biology of Belief* by Dr Bruce Lipton. This book should be compulsory reading for all medical students. Dr Lipton is a well respected specialist in the field of genetics, lecturing on the topic at medical school and without doubt a mainstream scientist. His research into genes led him to question the accepted medical paradigm that we are stuck with our genes and that there's nothing we can do to affect them.

When the Human Genome Project discovered that the entire human genome consists of about 25,000 genes – not the 120,000 that scientists were expecting – and that humans only have 1,500 more genes than a roundworm, and about the same as rodents, a shift in scientific understanding started to occur. A new branch of science, Epigenetics, meaning control above genetics, discovered that genes are not destiny. They found that environmental influences, like stress, nutrition and emotions can modify genes without changing the basic blueprint, which can then be passed on to future generations. [2]

So what has this got to do with the Mind? Everything, particularly when it comes to beliefs and mindset. For years diseases like cancer were put down to our genes. In fact, only 5% of cancer and cardiovascular disease is due to genetics. These and others like diabetes, are mainly lifestyle diseases and therefore avoidable if we look after ourselves, which of course the majority of us don't!

In his book, Dr. Lipton scientifically proves that our genes and the state of our health are very much influenced by the environment around the cells in our bodies. What he means is that the stories (Beliefs) we are unconsciously telling ourselves in our heads create the negative emotions and therefore the negative environments around the cells for disease to flourish: *The Biology of Belief.*

This helps explain why some people beat cancer and others don't. It explains the spontaneous remissions we often hear about, when doctors often apologise for misdiagnosis because that's the only seemingly possible explanation. We can affect the health of our cells with the thinking of our Minds.

The power of belief is shown by the placebo effect, which many people know about these days. It can be incredibly powerful. An article by Nieme in 2009 in *Scientific American Mind* described a meta-analysis of studies which measured the placebo effect in medicine. The results showed that placebo therapy worked for 40% of patients with Irritable Bowel Syndrome (IBS), 36-44% with duodenal ulcers and between 11% and 50% for patients with Multiple Sclerosis. [3]

This research has absolutely massive implications for healthcare moving forwards into the 21st century, but only if mainstream science is prepared to accept it. If scientific studies have proved that the placebo effect is often as effective as the drugs being tested, then surely the biggest challenge for science is to discover <u>why</u> the placebo effect is so effective. If we understood that, then medicine would be far less dependent on medication and drugs, which, given that drug side effects are reported as the second biggest cause of death in the U.S., would save millions of lives.

Dr. Lipton describes how in 1952, a young British doctor helped cure a boy of a lethal genetic disease, called Ichthyosis, using hypnosis. Hypnosis had often been used to cure warts; in fact, the doctor initially thought he was treating warts. By reversing the symptoms of Ichthyosis the doctor and the boy had achieved something that was until then considered medically impossible.

The doctor was then sent loads of patients with this apparently incurable disease. However, he was unable to replicate the results and he put the failure down to his own lack of belief in the treatment. When he thought he was treating a bad case of warts, his attitude was 'cocky' as though the treatment couldn't

> fail. But when he found out that he was actually treating something the medical profession considered to be incurable, his attitude changed. His new patients detected this at an unconscious level, even though he was 'acting' as certain as he could. [4]

This means that in certain scenarios, somebody's belief (i.e. Mind) can create physical changes in somebody else's body. The implications of this are literally mind blowing and yet the whole episode has been buried by the medical profession.

Recently, however, some mainstream researchers have turned their attention to the placebo effect. An article was published in 2002 in the *New England Journal of Medicine* by Dr. Bruce Moseley and colleagues, evaluating different methods of treating severe knee pain through surgery. They split the patients into 3 groups:

- One group had the damaged cartilage shaved

- Another had the knee area flushed out, removing any material thought to be causing the inflammation

- The last group had fake surgery. The patient was sedated and had three standard incisions, whilst Moseley talked and acted exactly as though he was carrying out real surgery, but simply sewed the incisions back up without doing anything.

Post operative care was identical for all three groups and guess what? The placebo group, who had nothing done to their knees, improved just as much as the other two groups! This is ultimate proof of the power of the Mind over the body. The most important issue science has to research today is how does the placebo effect work? It could provide the most cost efficient and side effect free possible therapeutic methodology.

> In another case, a man was taking part in a blind trial for a revolutionary new drug in the 'fight against' cancer. He was in the placebo group but was delighted with the efficacy of the new drug as he beat his cancer. Unfortunately, he read in the newspaper two years later that the drug was deemed an absolute failure. His cancer came back within weeks.
>
> So his rather 'creative' doctor asked if he wanted to be put down for the trial on the new improved version of the drug. Naturally he said yes and proceeded to recover with more placebo medication. He later read that the drug had finally been denied a patent and was not being launched onto the market. Unfortunately, the cancer beat him on the third occasion.

The opposite of placebo also exists: nocebo. In a Discovery Health Channel programme, an American doctor diagnosed a patient in 1974 with cancer of the oesophagus which was considered to be 100% fatal at the time. It was not a great surprise that the patient died a few weeks after his diagnosis. What was a surprise was that the autopsy, shortly after the patient's death, showed no trace of oesophageal cancer! If he didn't die of oesophageal cancer, what did he die of? The belief that he was going to die? [5]

People in positions of authority (doctors, teachers, parents) can accidentally remove hope and programme people to think that they are helpless. Telling somebody that depression will always be in their life - something many of my clients have been told by their doctors - is a prison sentence, but telling them they have three months to live is a death sentence.

Hypnotherapists and NLP practitioners are trained to understand the power of language and the need to keep it clean! Doctors, with their symbols of authority (white coats and stethoscopes) need similar training - the wrong words can be very damaging to life!

We know that 33% of all medical healings are due to the placebo effect, but how much illness and disease might be caused by the nocebo effect? Probably 70%, because psychologists estimate that 70% of our thoughts are negative and repetitive. So, used negatively our Beliefs can kill us, used positively, they can save our lives. These are of course dramatic examples, but it nevertheless puts the stories we tell ourselves (I'm useless, worthless and hopeless) into a different context.

The power of Belief is huge and as one of the main filters of the two million bits of information coming into our system every second, is responsible for a lot of the misery people find themselves in. Discovering our Limiting Beliefs is crucial to moving our lives forward, because we can change the way we see our lives unfolding.

Chapter 9:

Mental Autopilot

> *"The unexamined life is not worth living."*
>
> **Socrates**

Emotional Programming

We are not consciously in control of our emotions. We can't tell ourselves to be happy! Our emotions tend to get triggered automatically, often before we've had the chance to realise!

And the same things tend to trigger particular emotions time after time, anger is probably the most obvious one. By and large, our emotions run on autopilot! And typical behavioural responses to these emotional programmes are simply automated behavioural programmes!

Until recently scientists thought that the mid twenties signalled the end of the brain's ability to grow and change. By that age, they believed everything was literally 'hardwired'. In fact, the human brain is very neuroplastic which means that by continuously learning new information and by having new experiences, we adapt our behaviour and so continue reshaping the brain through our adult years. This means we can change many unconscious programmes ourselves by gaining the understanding and making them conscious.

The new brain, the neocortex, is the most plastic part, as its specific function is learning and conscious awareness.

So this is the area where we grow new neural patterns and change existing ones. The neocortex is being constantly reconfigured. [1]

This means we can change our programming. There are two ways to change our neural patterns or autopilot programming. Firstly, we can learn new things and secondly, we can have new experiences. Every time we learn something, the brain changes. I believe that this is why many of my clients make the changes they are looking for simply by understanding The Mind Matrix ©. You may remember the client in Chapter 8 who had the phobia of cold and lumpy food - she lost the phobia before coming back for formal therapy. She simply created a new neural circuit that made the old one about being insane untenable.

Our repeated Emotional Programming (for example, depression) is intimately tied up with our past experiences through our five senses. Our five senses record all of the incoming data from experiences - especially when they are new – and what we are seeing, hearing, feeling, smelling and even tasting during an event all gets recorded in our mind. The particular nature of the experience will dictate what hormone gets released. If we've just walked out in front of a car, it'll be adrenalin and cortisol for fight or flight; if we're lying blissfully and peacefully on a beach, then it'll be dopamine.

The hormones become intimately part of that particular experience. In other words, feelings are chemical memories. When we remember a particular experience we get the same feelings we had with the original experience. So with a constant negative feeling like depression, we are continually putting ourselves down and remembering other times when we've felt worthless, useless and hopeless and this in turn produces the negative hormones which cause the depressive feelings. We get caught in a habitual trap of negative emotion.

This autopilot function is reinforced by the way we learn. When we are learning something new there is inevitably a weak pattern of neural connection, because we haven't practised it yet. The way we learn is to join the weak pattern of neural connection with a stronger one, one we've already practised.

We learn in this way through the use of metaphor. If I'm describing the state of being in hypnosis to a new client, I will describe it as that feeling when we first wake up in the morning, being somewhere in limbo between being awake and asleep. The client doesn't know what hypnosis feels like yet, but he does know that snoozy, early morning feeling. In his mind, the feeling of hypnosis is now linked with the feeling of sleep, through The Law of Association. [2]

If we initially learn through The Law of Association, we remember through The Law of Repetition. To consciously remember every detail of something complex, like how to play a perfect forehand in tennis, is pretty much impossible. This is why top athletes practise their art time after time after time. By constantly repeating the same shot over and over again on the practice court, the tennis player is literally creating a muscle memory of how to play the shot.

This means that when he or she is in competition, there doesn't need to be any conscious thought to play the shot. The more we repeat an action, the more we reinforce the thought and the stronger the unconscious neurological connection becomes.

If we are having new experiences and learnings, then our old wiring is being abandoned and replaced with new patterns through Association and then reinforced with Repetition.

When we are unconsciously repeating the same thought patterns every day, the neural connections and the associated feelings and hormones, become automatic, routine and even familiar. We start to automatically and habitually think of ourselves in the same way. The more we repeatedly unconsciously think the same patterns and feel the same feelings, the more unconscious we become. Most of us spend a huge part of the day unconsciously thinking of and feeling old memories, because they have become hardwired autopilot programming.

The constant repetition of the neural connections means that they very easily become everyday thoughts and soon turn up as a voice in our heads telling us what to do and what not to do, how to feel and how not to feel. So the more we think certain things, the more we'll think of those things!

Often, because of The Law of Association, it only takes one stimulus from the environment to set off a conditioned set of automatic behaviours and responses. We don't need to think how to feel or think, our reactions seem normal because we've done it this way so often.

Our very ways of learning through the Laws of Association and Repetition are what create our unconscious emotional programming. It's easy to see why we accidentally create and then repetitively use negative, unwanted programmes. Often conscious understanding and simple awareness is enough to collapse them, though sometimes we need to work on a deeper level.

Neural Recoding, outlined in Chapter 11, is a wonderful aid to working on a deeper level on your own, if you need it. If the issues run deeper (like serious depression, burn-out and panic attacks), then you need to consult a therapist. Neural Recoding, done at home, is not a replacement for therapy and if you are at all unsure as to whether an issue is serious or not, you should definitely seek medical advice first.

Mind Chatter

For most of us, our mental autopilot produces Mind Chatter. It's the 'voice in the head', it's the constant internal commentator on our life. In fact, some people are aware of different voices. There's often the disapproving voice of our mother or one of our school teachers. Of course, we'd have been locked away in an asylum until recently, if we'd admitted that there was a voice in our head, but everybody has at least one.

However, the voice is rarely positive and, what is worse, psychologists reckon that the majority of 'self talk' is exactly the same content every day. But then when you consider the extent of our habitual and emotional programming, this is hardly a great surprise! How often does your voice say: "you're amazing Fred, well done"? It's more likely to be saying: "You're hopeless, you should have done better". If you now think about what your internal voice is telling you most of the time, you'll most likely agree that it's not making much of a positive contribution to your life.

Some people are so aware of their internal commentator that the voice begins to take on a personality. I had a lovely client called Chloe who came to see me for anorexia. Her voice was a Gestapo guard and she was scared of it and always listened to and obeyed the guard, particularly with regard to what she could and couldn't eat. She had a mental picture of the guard and would have a conversation with her. Chloe was not in the slightest bit insane, the guard was simply part of her mental processing.

The internal commentator is the one who's telling us that we've got to say something when we're sitting in the pub with our mates, otherwise, they'll think we're pathetic. When we're suffering from lack of Self Esteem, it's the internal commentator that will insist on planning every word of a point we want to make in a meeting at work. However, by the time we've worked out what we want to say to the last letter, the conversation's moved on and what we were going to say is no longer relevant!

Unfortunately the more stressed we are, the louder and more insistent the voice is. Most of the time, we're not actually aware of the voice, it's just under conscious awareness. But with a bit of practice, we can become much more aware of the internal commentary and stop it. When we do this, it gives us the chance to stand back and analyse what our Mind is up to on its own. We can then decide whether to listen to it or disregard it.

One of the tasks I give many of my clients when they leave my office is literally to stop the negative voice each time they're aware of it. As soon as we 'spot' the voice, it stops. To start with, that may be every five minutes. But the more we become aware of the negative voice and the more often we interrupt its personal commentary, the quieter the voice becomes.

Looking back at The Mind Matrix © and the filtering system, it's not surprising that the filters often clash or fight each other, causing Mind Chatter. Imagine if our Childhood Programming instilled in us the need for independence, which means we will have learnt to stand on our own two feet. If at the same time as independence, one of our greatest Values is love, friendship and community, our filtering system is set up for major conflict, and yes, I have often come across this exact filtering set-up with a number of clients. If, as a result of the need for independence, we have a commitment problem, we are likely to have a nasty relationship break-up.

This can easily lead to negative, depressive thinking and into major Mind Chatter. And as if all that weren't bad enough, two million bits of information a second go through this particular filtering arrangement.

I liken such chaotic filtering to a pinball machine. The ball comes round the chute at the top of the machine at some speed and starts to descend the slope. On its way down it gets catapulted in random directions by seemingly strategically placed buffers. We, as the operator, have little control over where the ball flies off to until it arrives at the bottom at the 'flippers,' over which we do have control. Then, with a certain amount of expertise and practice we can keep the ball in play.

With an unconsciously conflicting filtering system, different thoughts bounce off each filter onto the next, just like the ball descending the pinball machine, resulting in major Mind Chatter. The more filters that conflict and the more often these conflicts arise inside our heads, the louder the Mind Chatter.

For most of us, until we learn better, this process happens automatically. We don't realise that we have control of the flippers, so the ball just drops through the bottom into the Mind Chatter pit in the belly of the machine.

When we get a handle on our filters, the power is taken out of the metaphorical barriers and the ball flies around less, in other words, the Mind Chatter volume is turned down. What actually happens is that when we have the conscious understanding, the Unconscious Mind starts to move the filters and streamline the filtering system, without us knowing.

We will find ourselves letting go of Limiting Beliefs, our Values begin to change, we start to care less about what society thinks, we drop childhood rules and the pinball can drop through to its destination without unnecessary buffering!

To a large degree this happens unconsciously because after all, the Unconscious Mind's job is to keep us safe and happy. When it understands that the existing filtering system is causing pain, it will make changes and the only way this can happen is through conscious understanding.

What is more, when we find the filters changing, our behaviour changes, again often unconsciously. We start to take action and make changes in our lives and this makes us feel happier. We're taking control and life is changing. In fact, taking action to change our lifestyle is a critical part in making the changes permanent. Taking action in our life is the equivalent to taking control of the flippers on the pinball machine! We can stay happily and rewardingly in the game! These Filtering System changes can happen very quickly.

 Sarah's Story *Revisited*:

You'll remember Sarah from Chapter 4 whose number one and two Values were Freedom and Excitement. In her home background, her father was a successful businessman for whom success and making money were very important. He worked literally seven days a week, but two separate months of the year they took off on holiday as a family. They went to far off exotic locations like Tibet, Brazil and Egypt, and Sarah and her brothers had huge amounts of freedom and, of course, excitement.

The Childhood Programming that Sarah unconsciously took from this was that she too had to make lots of money and go on exotic holidays in order to achieve her freedom and excitement. When she came to see me she had, of course, just left home and become financially independent. The problem was that she was at the beginning of her career with an appropriate salary to boot! Not surprisingly, she was struggling to fund the exotic holidays.

So she began working harder and harder, just like her dad, to advance her career and earn more money. The problem was that unlike her dad, who, as an entrepreneur, immediately saw the returns from his hard work, she earned a salary. In fact, she didn't even receive a bonus, so it didn't matter how hard she worked, she couldn't earn more money to fund her expensive excitement and freedom.

After talking to her Dad about her discoveries, she found another two crucial jigsaw pieces. Firstly, her dad was incredibly proud of her and what she had achieved and secondly and most telling, all his hard work and money didn't make him happy. The two months a year were great, but they came at too big a cost in terms of his day to day relationship with his family. He'd learnt this lesson rather abruptly when Sarah (the eldest sibling) left home to find her own way in the world.

When we can consciously start to understand the unconscious forces that are driving our emotions and our habits, our goals and our desires, and can gain the understanding of how these subtle, but powerful forces can fight each other, causing emotional conflict and Mind Chatter, then our Unconscious will start to adapt the filtering system automatically. This not only allows us, but also drives us, to make changes in our lives.

Making changes does not have to be a long drawn out or painful process. For the majority of people, getting the life they want is a question of understanding the unconscious currents of the filtering system.

For others it's not quite so simple - there may be issues that need 'fixing'! The grief of losing a loved one can go on for years until the Unconscious finally lays the pain to rest. Being abused or badly bullied at school can leave enduring, but healable, scars, as can an abusive relationship. Those whose unresolved filtering clashes have led them into depression will also need a helping hand. But the Unconscious can release emotional pain caused by past injustices very quickly. Years of counselling are not necessary for most people.

Once they've understood how they are creating their unhappiness, they can easily believe that change is round the corner and the rest is simple: taking action as a result of the filtering changes. Change your Mind, Change your Life!

Imagination and Hallucination

Now that we've understood a little more about Mind Chatter and that continuous commentator in the head, I need to point out that the Mind Chatter is not one dimensional! What do I mean by that? Well, it's not actually JUST a voice in the head, the internal communication goes much deeper than that! Here comes the most important piece of information in this book. If you only understand this bit and take it with you, it alone will be worth the purchase cost!

The Unconscious Mind does not know the difference between imagination and reality. I'll say that again. The Unconscious does not know the difference between what we're imagining and what is actually happening. The Conscious Mind knows the difference of course, but the Unconscious doesn't work on this plane!

This is really what is at the bottom of Panic Attacks and Fears and Phobias. It isn't to say that the person who suffers from these is over-reacting and making things up, but most of the time they are reacting to their imagination. To some degree, fears and phobias make sense from a programming point of view. They are merely the Unconscious protecting the person from a perceived threat. However, the panic reaction is most regularly "fired off" when the threat" isn't actually there.

📖 Jane's Story:

Jane came to see me with a fear of rats. She now had an urgent need to sort it out: she was off on a gap year to India!

Normally phobias are caused by a trigger event. So for Jane that would have been a nasty experience with a rat. However it transpired she'd never even seen a live rat, she'd only seen them on the first Indiana Jones film.

Her fear was based completely in her imagination!

I hope you're getting your head around the difference, it's important! Here's an example to make it easier. Let's say you go to the fair and hop on a 'big wheel'. Your Unconscious doesn't know whether you're actually fifty feet up in the air on the big wheel or sitting at home on the sofa, imagining you're at the fair on the big wheel. Obviously your Conscious knows where you are...but your Unconscious doesn't. It simply doesn't work that way.

Now if that sounds completely wacky, this is the sort of thing scientists can now prove with Functional MRI scanning. This new technology maps the oxygenation of the blood flow in the brain. It enables them to see which part of the brain 'lights up' when we're thinking of or experiencing different things. So the same parts of the brain will light up whether we are actually fifty foot up in the air on the Big Wheel or whether we are at home imagining it. The Unconscious doesn't know the difference.

What if?

So how is this relevant to the Mind Chatter? Well, most of us spend the time in our heads worrying about the future. What if this happens? Or what if that happens? Well, as soon as you say to yourself "What if?" you go straight into imagination and by definition, the thing you're imagining hasn't happened yet!

Guess what? Most of the Mind Chatter is pure imagination. It hasn't happened, only the Unconscious doesn't know that because it doesn't know the difference between imagination and reality. So as far as the Unconscious is concerned, the imagined situation has already happened or is happening right now!

Let's give you an example to illustrate what's going on, an example that's very relevant to a lot of people in the current state of the economy: "What if I lose my job?" That's a big one that a lot of people are battling with in their heads at the moment.

We start by asking ourselves that simple question: "What happens if I lose my job?" But the thinking doesn't stop there! That's too one dimensional for the Unconscious! We soon go a level deeper into imagination and ask ourselves: "What happens if I can't pay the bills?" And then a level deeper: "What if I can't pay the mortgage?" Then we go yet another level deeper: "What happens if we lose the house?"

Before you know it, your Mind's making a picture of all of your belongings out on your front lawn with the bailiffs starting to help themselves. Hang on a minute! You haven't lost your job. See what I mean? How easy it is to get carried away with the hallucination of the Mind Chatter? This is what I call Layered Thinking and it's something the Unconscious does very easily It's very destructive and easily leads to anxiety and even depression.

The Fight or Flight Response

The real problem here is that it's also the Unconscious that manages our hormonal system. I'm thinking particularly of the 'Fight or Flight Response' that by now most people have heard of. The Fight or Flight Response was wonderful when we were living in caves. Just imagine walking around the corner and there's a sabre-toothed tiger. Our life is in danger, so the Fight or Flight Response is activated in a split second; all the blood goes to our arms and our legs with a sudden surge of adrenalin, cortisol and noradrenalin, ready for us to fight or run like hell! Once we've fought the sabre-toothed tiger (and killed it) or successfully run away, we've used up and burnt off all the adrenalin, cortisol and noradrenalin and everything returns to normal.

How often do we see a sabre-toothed tiger today? How often is our life **actually** in danger? Pretty much never! The nearest a few of us get is something like stepping off the pavement without thinking in front of a car. We get a sudden shot of adrenalin and find ourselves back on the pavement breathing incredibly fast and dripping with sweat. That's our good old Unconscious Mind doing its stuff. No time for thinking, or we would have been run over!

Today's life threats are not real life threats though, our lives aren't actually in danger. They are lifestyle threats. Unfortunately, our Unconscious and our hormonal system act as though they are genuine life or death situations. We experience the Fight or Flight Response, even if we are just imagining that we've lost our job. It's not good news, but our lives are not actually in danger!

The next problem is, how can we physically run away from or fight losing our jobs? We can't, so all the adrenalin, cortisol and noradrenalin remains locked up in our system because we can't burn it off. Well, guess what? Excess levels of adrenalin, cortisol and noradrenalin are poisonous. Yes, our body manufactures poison! When you accidentally walk in front of a car and then find yourself on the pavement within a second -. something pretty dramatic has to happen in our bodies to get that sort of reaction!

In the short term, the cortisol enables us to release dopamine, which keeps us alert. This is useful of course if we need prolonged alertness (i.e. more than the Fight or Flight Response), but it is poisonous and harms both the brain and the body if it stays activated for too long. With excess levels of these 'poisonous' hormones in our system, we remain 'jittery' and fire off the Fight or Flight mechanism even more easily in the future, sending ourselves into a potential chemical spiral. This unconscious spiral is the basis of most of our so-called modern diseases - stress, anxiety and depression.

Early humans didn't have to worry about terrorism or nuclear war, the dangers they faced were much more immediate – starvation or being set upon by a larger predator. However, the neural connection and hormone rushes that automatically take place when the Fight or Flight Response is triggered, haven't changed. Moreover, through The Law of Repetition, these thought patterns, having been fired over hundreds of thousands of years, are all too readily available to us!

But due to advances in technology and social structures, our concerns are different today. We are under time pressure sitting in a traffic jam, we're worried about paying the mortgage or credit card debts, we're worried about losing our jobs, or we're caught up in political chicanery at work. The problem is that the Fight or Flight Response works physiologically the way it always has and it is now triggered far more frequently. In fact, for most of us, several times a day!

Because the new 'life threats' are so frequent, we spend much of our time in anticipatory mode, imagining the dangers, and our system fires off, just as though the dangers were real! Our large neocortices have the ability to imagine and we are very good at anticipating dangers and, even though they are not real (the dangers haven't actually happened yet), our habituated thought patterns fire off the Fight or Flight Response.

We've learned to anticipate dangers particularly well in times of uncertainty. Our imagination is capable of coming up with all sorts of life threatening scenarios and making these imagined scenarios all the more convincing because we can associate them with real life threatening situations in the past.

This means that we spend a significant amount of time in survival mode with adrenalin and cortisol coursing round our bodies. Being continually on red alert mode, our body doesn't have the time to repair itself. Unlike most other animals, we have the ability to trigger the Fight or Flight Response with our imagination and because we can't fight or run away from worries about bills and mortgages, the adrenalin and cortisol gets locked in our system.

In addition, one of the things we face daily is change, the speed of which is accelerating dramatically. Change means uncertainty and uncertainty means that we unconsciously begin to anticipate possible dangers and trigger off our Fight or Flight Response. Our evolutionary advantage in being able to anticipate danger has also become our Achilles' heel. Used positively, our imagination is perhaps our strongest asset as a species, but used negatively, it's our biggest weakness!

Human beings experience three types of stress: physical (a car accident, an injury, lack of sleep, food or water); chemical (toxins, allergens, pollutants); emotional (worries over time, money, relationships). Our system reacts the same way whichever type of stress we experience. Virtually all animals' stress experiences are limited to physical stress.

Most of our stresses are emotional and can't be fought or run away from. For many of us this leads to chronic stress, where we are constantly bombarded by things and people that stress us out. Because we can't run away, we are left to worry, analyse and then imagine virtually all day long. There's no running away from chronic stress!

More worrying still is the fact that emotional stress causes physical stress. Most people are walking around with tension in their shoulders, which in turn produces chemical stress (the adrenal response that stays locked in our system). The chemical stress then produces more physical stress because our bodies can't regenerate or repair, so the tension in our shoulders just gets worse and downwards the spiral goes!

The Health and Safety Executive (HSE) in the UK estimates that 75% of doctors' visits are due to stress. Chronic stress, the continuous state of red alert, is what really does the damage. Our bodies weren't built to cope with long term stress and we haven't had the chance to evolve physically or mentally yet to deal with it.

Sadly, this modern version of the Fight or Flight Response is leading most of us to an early grave. Continually high residual levels of adrenalin and cortisol break down our immune system, laying us much more open to serious disease, such as cancer and heart disease. No wonder these diseases are skyrocketing. And of course, people with chronic stress double the size of the problem because they can't sleep, missing the critical part of the day when the body regenerates.

Stress also impairs our basic cognitive functions and there's a huge correlation between chronic stress and depression. Stress plays havoc with our blood sugar levels leading to adult onset diabetes and obesity. It compromises our digestion too, because the Fight or Flight Response sends the blood supply to the limbs and away from the stomach which can lead to IBS (Irritable Bowel Syndrome) and constipation.

How many of us answer "yes" to the following?

- Always exhausted

- Depressed

- Lack of energy

- Poor sleep patterns

- Frequent colds and flu

- Foggy thinking

- Digestive problems

- Backaches

- Weight problems

Isn't this the health profile of the average westerner? And the cause (and the solution) for all of this is in our heads!

What is worse, because we're not burning off the adrenalin, cortisol and noradrenalin and it remains floating around in our system, we're already more stressed and will more easily fire off the Fight or Flight Response for the next unnecessary situation! And the more easily we fire it off, the more adrenalin, cortisol and noradrenalin builds up in our system and the more easily we fire it off the next time, and so on!

Layered Thinking

And guess what? This whole spiralling process of Layered Thinking is an hallucination! It all started with our imagination, but our Unconscious doesn't know that! It's a very simple process. We imagine losing our jobs, our Unconscious spirals into pictures and feelings of unemployment and worse, our Fight or Flight Response is fired off and we can't do anything about it. So the poisonous hormones get locked in our bodies, we get more and more anxious until we descend into panic attacks, stress, anxiety or depression.

People are more likely to suffer depression if they succumb easily to negative thoughts when their mood is low, and they then dwell on the negative thoughts, trying to understand them. Depressed people believe that by thinking their negative thoughts through (why they feel like this, where the negative thoughts came from) they will be able to reduce or even beat their pain. But the thinking is counter productive because it keeps the negative thoughts in the mind and the more a person thinks about them, the more they are there. Emotions are kept in the Unconscious Mind, so logical, rational, conscious thinking is not the answer because it perpetuates the depressive feelings by keeping the negative thoughts alive.

Unsolved depression recurs because the sufferer reconnects with depressive feelings from past episodes when their mood is low. Regular negative thinking creates a pattern or 'groove' within the Mind, which becomes easier and easier to return to the more it is used. Reactivation of the thought patterns becomes automatic, it goes onto Autopilot as Emotional Programming. It is certainly not a deliberate conscious choice, indeed it is the last thing the sufferer wants.

The Emotional Programming is made deeper by the fact that the body reacts to the negative thinking with feelings and physical sensations, rather than just thoughts. If not dealt with, the Emotional Programming can become an ongoing state of mind that becomes a full relapse into depression. It's the thinking that causes depression! In addition the body reacting physically to negative thoughts is especially important with regards to cancer.

> ### 📖 Claire's Story:
>
> Claire was diagnosed with terminal cancer in July 2012. Claire is a dynamic lady and rather than accept her fate, she decided to do some research to do everything she could to beat the cancer.
>
> She is supporting her chemo treatment with Immunotherapy. Whilst chemo kills cancer cells, it also kills the person's immune system, so it makes total sense to do anything that can support the immune system.
>
> Claire came to see me, because part of her research had shown how critical keeping a positive mindset is to supporting the immune system and hence beating cancer. Not surprisingly she was prone to having morbid thoughts and was struggling with Self Esteem.
>
> It is particularly important for Claire to remain upbeat because she runs a blog on cancer (**www.triplenegative.co.uk/blog/**). She is a fantastic role model for people with cancer (or any other life-threatening illness) and is a very special lady! She laughed this off as me suggesting she had "special needs"... typical Claire!

One of the ways the human Mind deals with so much information, is that it instantly makes comparisons between things as they are right now and past similar situations. Thus, when our current reality is not how we want it to be (i.e. we're sad) the Mind creates a 'gap' between how things are and how we want them to be. This 'gap' automatically triggers negative thinking and sets in motion the thinking processes to reduce the gap. Unfortunately, thinking won't reduce the gap, only taking action will. If action is taken, then the Mind will have to come out of the 'Thinking Mode' in order to complete the action. [3]

When we're feeling down, our typical reaction is to try and get rid of the 'nasty' feelings; we try to bury them or worse, try to think our way out of them. As part of that thinking process, we drift away from the present moment, as we think of similar bad times from the past and then wonder how bad things might be in the future.

This is not a deliberate choice, it's an unconscious programme. We try out lots of different solutions in our heads to sort things out and, when we fail to come up with the right solution, we beat ourselves up for failing to solve the problem. We spend the whole time comparing where we are now with where we want to be and we spend the whole time completely in our heads.

We can become totally preoccupied with 'sorting ourselves out', losing touch with the real world, even with those that we love. We can spiral down and down until we've moved completely away from reality and live our lives in a dream, or rather a nightmare, in our heads, and it's not real. Since we can't seem to sort things out in this nightmare world, we start to lose hope that we'll ever be happy again.

We've become very goal orientated in our thinking, not just at work, but in our private lives. By clinging to the goals, even if they are good ones, we set up the 'gap analysis' that leads to the downward spiral of negative thinking. It's the desperate need, especially for us conscientious folks, to work towards and achieve a goal that keeps us in a state of unhappiness.

There is no readily available logical solution, so the Mind goes round and round trying to find it. This cycle will continue until something urgent takes the attention. However, once the urgent issue is dealt with, the thinking cycle will return. The focus on the 'gap' inevitably leads to a feeling of things being unsatisfactory, quickly followed by a feeling of inadequacy, because we can't beat it. Because there is no immediately available solution, the Mind remains locked in 'Thinking Mode'. With repetition, these negative thoughts come to be experienced as 'real', rather than thinking.

These layered thinking patterns are based on well rehearsed emotional programming that consists of the following:

- Autopilot

- Constantly monitoring the 'gap' between current reality and how we would like it to be

- A desire to be perpetually happy and get rid of negative moods and feelings

- A total reliance on rational, conscious thinking.

The answer to getting out of the layered thinking patterns is to learn to let the constant thinking go, freeing ourselves from the continual gap analysis. It's about accepting that things aren't great right now and occupying ourselves with positive action - taking exercise, seeing friends (and not moaning!) or doing something to improve our lives.

Ruby Wax explains this clearly: "Only with regular exercise of bringing awareness to negative thoughts and feelings will you be able to break those mental and physical habits... You have lots of opportunities to practice on your stress and you'll fail many times but just by altering your attention, you're creating new patterns of behaviour. Each time we face our feelings head-on rather than run, we're building muscle just like any sportsman when practicing his skills."

Her book explains Mindfulness, which is about becoming aware of the body and using that as a means to calm the

Mind Chatter, in great detail and in very understandable terms: " You're being kind to yourself by intentionally moving your attention from the mind to the body. Your body can withstand emotions; your mind can't because it's hard-wired to come up with a solution when there isn't one." [4]

The Reticular Activating System

There's one final (and rather lethal!) step in this unconscious Layered Thinking process! There's a certain part of our Mind called the Reticular Activating System or RAS. This is the part of the Mind that is (unconsciously) set up to look for what we want, it's like an antenna. However, when the Mind Chatter is loud, it looks for what we don't want!

The easiest way to explain this is to give you a couple of examples:

Have you ever bought a new car, been really proud of your new car, thinking it's really quite special and rare, only to find the same sort of car parked on every street corner? Well, those cars were there before, but because you didn't own one, your RAS wasn't set up to notice them.

Another example is that pregnant women see other pregnant women everywhere, whereas a man can walk straight past a pregnant woman and not even notice that she's pregnant. His RAS isn't set up for that, whereas for the pregnant woman, her whole life is centred on being pregnant!

OK, so how does this relate to our hallucinated Layered Thinking? If I'm worried about losing my job and I'm flicking through the local paper, I see to my horror that the company just down the road has laid off 20 people. If I wasn't worried about losing my job, the chances are that I'd have skipped straight past that article without even noticing it. So if we keep telling ourselves how useless we are, guess what our RAS finds? Examples of how useless we are!!

However, the power (and worse, misdirection) of the RAS is not something trivial. It is a major part of our unconscious thinking processes and more often than not brings misery into our lives. It looks for and finds what we don't want and sends that information through the Mind Matrix © Filtering System for the whole process to start again. We go back into the spiralling negative feedback loop.

Often, it's the way we interpret something that happens, or something somebody has said, which starts the Layered Thinking process. The Mind automatically and unconsciously goes through a three step process in reacting to something. Step 1 is the reality, the facts of the situation. Step 2 is the interpretation we give to the situation, that is, the story about the situation that we tell ourselves and is normally just below conscious awareness. Step 3 is our reaction to the situation in the form of feelings and behaviour. We are not usually aware of Step 2. We go straight from the situation to our reaction, without realising that we've interpreted the situation according to our own ways of thinking and that's what our reaction is based on. [5]

But thanks to neuroplasticity, we can change the way our brain is wired. In fact, the neocortex, the part of the brain responsible for reasoning and thinking, is particularly malleable in this respect. It changes with each new piece of learning and each new experience. This can happen positively, just as much as it can negatively.

We need to train the Mind to become more aware of our own personal reaction to or interpretation of an event

(Step 2). We can do this by 'standing back', accepting the situation and not fighting it, even if it is not how we want it to be. This slight distance allows us the space to step aside from our normal routine of plunging into reams of logical thoughts about how to solve a situation and the consequent negative feelings leading to the downward spiral. It's what happens at that exact point between Step 1 and Step 2 that needs to change. This can be done with a change of attitude, by being nonjudgemental and being more connected with the world and reality, instead of disappearing off into our heads.

When we take on this attitude of awareness and acceptance and create the space, there are enormous benefits:

- We can get out of our heads and experience the world for what it really is, not via the stories we are creating in our heads

- We can recognise our thoughts as just that, thoughts, not reality, just a way of thinking. So thoughts about how useless and worthless I am are just ideas, not the truth

- We can stop disappearing off into the past or the future and live life now in all of its wonder

- We can switch off the Autopilot and the downward spiral of Layered Thinking

- We can stop trying to force life to conform to our own ideas about how it should be and step away from the incessant negative thinking

The space allows us to accept negative situations. For example, it's pouring with rain as we're shopping in town, so we rush into a doorway to avoid getting soaked. After a while it becomes clear that the rain is not going to stop for the foreseeable future so, like it or not, we're going to have to step into it and get wet. There are two ways we can approach this situation:

- We step into the rain swearing at the weather and imagining how uncomfortable and cold we're going to be and what our partner's going to say when we walk through the front door dripping onto the carpet.

- We can accept that it's raining and that we're going to get wet and as near as possible enjoy the experience, becoming aware of the freshness that rain brings. We arrive home wet, but not unhappy, greet our partner as they open the door for us and go and get changed without grumbling, because we couldn't have changed the weather anyway.

Crucially, bringing this unconscious process into Consciousness, each of us understanding what our own individual Filtering, Autopilot and Hallucination processes are, starts the breakdown of stuck and unwanted patterns. If we maintain the resulting Self Awareness and take action towards taking our life where we want it to be, then everything can change.

This is how The Happiness Hierarchy © works. By understanding how our own Unconscious works, we can gain Self Awareness. With Self Awareness, we can understand how we've been creating our misery, stress, anxiety etc, forgive ourselves and develop the Self Esteem that we deserve. When we feel good about ourselves, we don't have to be swayed by what others or society in general say, we can just be ourselves... Authentic. That is true happiness and real power to make change happen around you.

Chapter 10:
The Ladder of Change

> *"You find peace not by rearranging the circumstances of your life, but by realizing who you are at the deepest level."*
>
> **Eckhart Tolle**

So now you've had a chance to understand the unconscious emotional and behavioural programmes you have, the big question now is: "OK so where do I make changes in my life?" If you are not satisfied with the way your life is, then you must actively change something. However, making changes in the right place is essential. As you will see later in this chapter, making changes in the wrong place can make things even worse! This chapter provides a guiding structure, so that you can work out where to make those changes.

I have developed The Ladder of Change as an adaptation of the Logical Levels model developed by the great Robert Dilts, one of the real geniuses behind NLP.

There are basically five areas within which you can make changes in your life:

- Environment

- Capability

- Behaviour

- Identity

- Consciousness

If you want to be happy, fulfilled and successful and want to change something, it's essential you make the change at the right level. The reason I call it The Ladder of Change is that the lower down the Ladder you are (Environment being the lowest), the bigger the effort and time required to make the change; the higher up the Ladder you are, sometimes all that's needed is a slight tweak! But when you've made the change, big or small, your whole life changes!

The easiest way to explain the Ladder is to give you examples of past clients to illustrate what I mean.

Environment

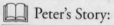 **Peter's Story:**

I saw Peter when he had lost his wife under rather unpleasant circumstances about two years prior to coming to see me. He was functioning OK, going to work and so on, but he had no real energy or enthusiasm. His real problem was that he came home every night, opened the front door and the grief descended on him within minutes and this had happened every night for two years.

I quickly established that he hadn't moved house since his wife had died. In fact, his wife's clothes were still in the wardrobe. I asked whether he could move house. After a little consideration, he said it would be rather difficult as his children went to the local school and all of their and his friends were local.

I then asked him how recently he'd redecorated the house. He replied that he left all of that to his wife, he didn't even lift a paintbrush! So nothing had changed since his wife had died. As well as helping him to let his wife go at an Unconscious level, I suggested that Peter needed to take some action to change things, his house was clearly an anchor for his grief. I asked him to consider redecorating the house from head to foot and making it his furniture, his colour schemes.

He agreed to do this. It took him about six months in all. Interestingly, I got a very excited email from him about a month into the process. His colleagues at work had noticed a real change in him. They said the 'old!' Peter was back. Where had he been?! Needless to say the nightly grief disappeared almost immediately. He was changing his Environment. Although it took six months to complete and a lot of money, the important thing was that afterwards every aspect of his life changed!

Other environment changes include moving house, moving job, getting married, getting divorced...

When a marriage starts to break down, it's quite common for people to make a change at the wrong level, which makes things even worse, for example, moving house. After the 'honeymoon period' of choosing fabrics, paint colours etc, everything settles back to normal and the relationship is just as bad as it ever was. Couples have also been known to have another child to help heal the marriage. Not that that's going to put any more stress on the already fragile relationship or anything!!

Is changing your environment (albeit quite a loose definition of what environment might mean) the right solution for you? Is the change being made at the right level of the Ladder?

Capability

Not many people need to make changes in their capability and if they do, it's normally glaringly obvious.

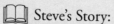 Steve's Story:

Steve came to see me about four years ago with depression. He'd tried counselling, but, like a lot of my clients, felt worse afterwards than when he started! He also found that anti-depressants weren't working.

After doing the Self Discovery Exercise with him, I found that he'd recently been promoted and wasn't coping very well. In fact, anybody who's ever been over promoted beyond their existing ability will know what a scary place this is! His company had made a classic 'Harvard Business School' case study error. Because Steve was a brilliant salesman and easily achieved his targets each month, they promoted him to Sales Manager. Unfortunately, Steve had managed nothing more complex than a guinea pig! Just because he was a good salesman, it didn't automatically make him a good Sales Manager.

After 3 months as Sales Manager, it became clear that the sales force of twelve was not being managed properly and that their sales were dropping badly.

Steve realised that this was his fault and started to lose his confidence. As his confidence dropped, his sales dropped too. His boss took him aside and asked whether he had a problem at home because he'd never missed his sales target in seven years. In fact, Steve did have a problem at home. He'd lost virtually all of his self confidence and his wife had lost respect for him too. No wonder he was depressed. In fact, in his words "[his] life had gone down the toilet in three months!" and he couldn't understand why. He hadn't made the connection between his lack of performance as a manager and his depression.

We worked on regenerating his previously healthy Self Esteem, but it was perfectly obvious that the long term solution was learning how to manage people and specifically a sales force. We found a Sales Management course at his local college, which was a day a week in college for 6 months and lots of homework. He learnt how to manage his sales force properly, their sales came back, his sales came back, his boss was happy, his wife was happy and his life was back. It took a fair bit of his time but changing his capability in that one area, transformed his whole life.

I was once over promoted for a job. I didn't have the requisite skills to do it. It's one of the scariest places I've ever been. I was continually looking over my shoulder, waiting for somebody to find me out. If I'd had the confidence at the time, I'd have put my hand up and asked to be sent on a course. Simple solution really and my employer would have got better value from me. Is there an area of your life where you don't feel capable? Could you learn that skill? What's stopping you?

Behaviour

The traditional view is that making changes in behaviour takes months if not years, but then counselling is not a speedy process! In my opinion, raking over old painful ground (which is how my clients tend to describe their experience of counselling) by talking things through, is a conscious activity, and because emotional problems are by definition lodged in the Unconscious, this is not always a good solution. The other 'modern' therapy for behavioural change is Cognitive Behavioural Therapy or CBT. CBT consists of teaching people strategies to manage their problems. A great example is Anger Management Classes. Anger Management classes make me angry! If I have an anger problem, why would I want to manage it?! I don't want the problem in the first place!

Dealing with anger properly means dealing with the cause or trigger at an Unconscious level. The original cause of the anger, often from childhood, needs to be brought into Consciousness and then dealt with... at an Unconscious level. I see most people for anger problems for two to three sessions and the person's behaviour changes very quickly.

📖 Tariq's Story:

There's a similar issue with Obsessive-Compulsive Disorder or OCD. Tariq came to see me eight years ago for OCD. He was a Cambridge post-graduate and had walked out of his third CBT class because he felt he was being patronised. It wasn't management strategies he wanted, he wanted a solution.

He came to my offices from Cambridge by taxi. At the end of the second session, I took him back to the waiting room and asked my P.A. to book him a taxi. Five minutes later my office door was thrown open and there stood Tariq in floods of tears. Fortunately, I quickly established that they were tears of joy. He'd gone to the toilet and come out in under a minute, and then burst into tears. Those of you familiar with OCD will probably be aware that a common behaviour of the OCD sufferer is the need to wash and rewash their hands fearing that germs remain on the hands. In common with many OCD sufferers, Tariq's hands were raw with continuous washing. He couldn't re-member the last time, he'd simply gone to the toilet, washed his hands and come out again. No wonder he was in tears.

A crucial part of changing your behaviour will be authenticating key relationships in your life.

Authenticating your existing Relationships

Very few of us have genuinely open and authentic relationships where we are totally honest and vulnerable. For most of us, this is especially so with our close relationships.

Now don't start beating yourself up! Look at the Cultural Programming outlined in Chapter 7. It's hardly surprising, when the world's so competitive, that the natural reaction is to protect ourselves, not to lay ourselves bare! You've just begun to understand your own Childhood Programming and the effect it's had on your life. Has that encouraged you to keep yourself safe or to be open, honest and vulnerable in your relationships? Of course it hasn't!

The problem is, the only way we can have a deep connection with others, is by being open, honest and vulnerable! It's no good hiding, avoiding, protecting! That's not being Authentic and won't make you happy!

So a massive step onto your path of Authenticity will be to clean up the relationships with "those that matter"! And now you understand the dynamics, why wouldn't you do that? It's freedom!

You'd be amazed what a difference it makes when you come clean and admit what you've been feeling, even if it's been unconscious until now. The first relationships to clean up are with your parents, because the chances are that your childhood decision involved them.

I know this sounds incredibly scary, if not suicidal! But believe me the outcome is well worth it. Or does this sound pointless because you have a fabulous relationship with your parents? Well, do you? Your childhood decision may say otherwise. I'm not talking about a civil and duty based relationship, I mean one where you can deeply share yourself.

Authenticating the Relationship with my Dad

I would like to share my story with you. It'll help you understand what I'm on about! My childhood decision was "I've got to do all this myself, I'm not worthy of being loved", taken at the tender age of 6 months!

I've been angry with my dad for 'packing me off' to boarding school at seven with very bad asthma, where I got pretty badly bullied. I then made another (unconscious childhood) decision which was to withdraw my love from my dad. This was compounded in later life when my business went bust and I all but fell apart. I've been angry (unconsciously because of the childhood decision) with him because 'he wasn't really there for me' at that time!

Think about my story, 'I've got to do all this myself'. Firstly, I'm pretty sure I didn't let anybody (including my dad or my wife) know how badly my business going bust had affected me and secondly, I am pretty certain my 55% unconscious communication would have been; "Don't offer me your help, I've got to do this on my own". How was he supposed to help with that going on?

I know this makes me sound callous, but I wasn't aware that I was withdrawing my love! If I'm really honest, my relationship with my dad for most of my life has been that civil duty based type and that was largely pretty much all down to my childhood decision. I've longed to connect with him properly but haven't known how to do it.

I do now! I rang my dad recently to tell him what I've worked out. The conversation went something like this:

Dad: "Hello"

Me: "Pa, I've rung up to tell you I love you".

At which point I promptly burst into tears, because I realised instantly that's probably the first time I've ever told him that! Not surprisingly there was a silence on the other end of the phone.

Me: "It's alright Pa, everything's OK. I haven't had a fatal accident, I'm not on drugs, nor have I joined a cult!"

Me: "I haven't rung for a long conversation and I don't want to get into one. I just want to share something with you that I've just worked out and then I want to put the phone down. I'll call you later for a longer chat"

Dad: "Ok". I could almost hear his thoughts: "Oh my God, what's coming!"

Me: "I've just realised that I've been unconsciously angry with you for forty five years for packing me off to boarding school at the age of seven with very bad asthma. As a result, it seems I made a childhood decision to withdraw my love from you and I'M SO SORRY!"

Additional floods of tears!

Dad:" Well, I think you're being a bit hard on yourself..."

Me: "Thanks Pa, but I don't need you to say anything I just wanted to get this off my chest"

Dad:"Well before you get off the phone, let me just let you know that you went to boarding school at ten and not seven. Also the only reason me and your mum were happy to let you go was because you were so excited about it".

Silence. At my end of the phone this time! You could have knocked me down with a feather. That's not how I remembered it at all!

Me: "Oh my God! Pa, I've got to digest that. I'll call you back later."

My Unconscious had changed history (in my head) so that I could justify my story!

There were two outcomes from that conversation:

- Already, I've got a much more open relationship with the most important man in my life! I've cleared the decks and know that I can be totally open, honest and vulnerable with him from now on. We ring each other more often (probably not often enough, but we're all so busy on our treadmills!) and I've allowed him to help me and I now listen avidly to his advice instead of thinking: "Stop lecturing me, I've got to do this on my own!" Let's face it, he's had more life experience than I have!

- I'm so proud to be his son. When I was bullied, he went straight into the school and tore a few shreds off the headmaster! I've never given him credit for that! At the age of thirty, he financed, designed and built (a lot of it with his own hands) our beautiful family home set in two acres of what was an old fruit farm. He has no formal architectural or construction training. My God, the thought of me trying to do that at thirty or even fifty two!!! At the age of sixty five he built himself a yacht and sailed round the world (most of it with a single crewman) for twenty months. I've never really given him the credit for that either. What an incredible man!

Before you leave this and think: "Thanks Mark, nice story", I promise you've got something similar going on. Wouldn't you benefit from cleaning up your most important relationships? Yes, it's scary when you first do it, but it's worth it. This is Authenticity and it takes so much of the fear out of your life. When you've cleaned up a relationship, you don't need to hide, avoid or blame anymore! Think of the mental energy you save!

If you're so excited that you want to get straight on the phone, just hang fire a couple of moments! Here's some absolutely essential advice, which you **must** heed!

Firstly, if you look at the conversation above, it was set up in a very careful way. This was about **me** taking responsibility for **my** childhood decision and behaviour. This was absolutely not about blaming my Dad for whatever might have been his part in all of this. I made it clear, I wanted to share something and get off the phone.

If you get into a conversation, there's a big danger that the other person will feel the need to start defending themselves and **this is not about blame.** There's no need for them to defend themselves.

So your desired outcome is to share something and get off the phone. Your longer term objective is to have an open relationship with that person. You're not going to get that if you allow the conversation to descend into an argument or the blame game!

So Behaviour can change very quickly, although not as quickly as Identity.

Identity

Identity is hugely important when it comes to happiness and fulfilment. Our sense of identity is how we perceive ourselves and our place in the world. It also includes our sense of purpose - why are we here? What is it that we should or could be doing with our lives? To help you expand your thoughts on this important topic, here's the story of a past client.

Patrick's Story:

Patrick came to see me just before Christmas 2008 with depression. He was a builder, so after an initial chat, I made the point that given that the building industry is always the first to collapse when there's a recession, I wasn't altogether surprised that he was feeling low.

His response was immediate: "Oh no mate! I know what you're saying, but when things get difficult normally, it pushes me harder to get the work in. Only this time, it doesn't make any sense anymore, I'm finding it hard to get out of bed. What's happened?"

I then asked him if he was a builder!

He looked at me puzzled and replied as though I was the one who needed help, "Yes I'm a builder."

"OK", I said, "if you're a builder, what is it that you enjoy about being a builder? Do you build a wall, stand back and then admire the workmanship?"

"Oh no mate", he says. "I get other people to do that work for me!" (The clue for me was the pin stripe suit and tie he was wearing!)

"OK then, are you a builder?"

Now he's starting to get angry, but he squeezes out the words, "Yes, I'm a builder!"

"So if it isn't the actual building work that you enjoy about being a builder, what do you enjoy?"

He's now sitting on the edge of his chair and talking excitedly: "Well it's the whole process, Mark. You wait months for the right project to come in and when one lands in your lap, you have to work really fast. You get the planners in and make sure that they're not building a motorway at the back in the next four years. Tick, that's done! Then you get the architects in and draw up the plans. I enjoy that bit, it's creative! Tick that's done! Then you get the legal boys in and you do the deal".

And he shoves his hand out towards me as he does the deal in his head. He's now grinning and amazingly animated. The sudden change in him nearly takes my breath away.

"OK," I say. "Are you a builder?"

"Yes, I'm a ****ing builder," he replies. "What are you getting at?"

"Well, who else does deals?" and I put my hand out, as though I'm doing a deal.

After a few seconds, he says, "Bankers!"

That wasn't quite the answer I was looking for, so I say, "OK final question. Who are your role models? Who do you look up to?"

"Oh Richard Branson, Duncan Bannatyne, Alan Sug... oh my God, I'm an entrepreneur!"

He gets ten 'eureka moments' in one go and it slams him into the back of the chair and he sits there dazed for two to three minutes. I let him process that, as I can see all sorts of things are going on in his head. Suddenly he gets out of his seat and walks towards the door.

"Hang on a minute," I say. "You've only been here ten minutes and you've paid for a four hour session."

"Forget it mate, best four hour session I've ever had" and walks out of the door! He changed his Identity in a five minute conversation. He was an entrepreneur not a builder!

He came back to see me after Christmas with a huge smile on his face. "You won't believe it, Mark" he said." I set up two companies over the Christmas period. And guess what? I spotted the first opportunity two years ago but let it go because I was a builder. I assumed some other lucky sod would do it! Even the other one, I spotted about 6 months ago, but again, it wasn't building, so I didn't do it! By the way, neither of the opportunities has got anything to do with building!"

I got an email from him in September 2009 (just nine months after he came to see me) telling me that one of companies was now making (not turning over) £40,000 a month. Of course it was: he's an entrepreneur!

At the end of the first session before Christmas he'd quite simply changed his identity, or how he saw himself, in a five minute conversation. Once he got used to the idea, he took action, and very successful he was too! By seeing himself solely as a builder, he was completely limiting his opportunities. Clearly he is a very bright guy and a very 'out of the box' thinker, both traits which were being squashed completely. By the way, the depression and lack of energy disappeared the same day as the first session!

Consciousness

Consciousness sounds very grand and complicated, but for the purposes of The Ladder of Change model, we'll define it simply as our way of thinking, particularly with regards to big and important issues.

 My Family Story:

The example here isn't as exciting as the last one, but it is very personal! About twelve years ago, my wife and I read an A4 sized article in *The Sunday Times* on the environmental impact of the average household, what is now called your carbon footprint. It only took us about two minutes to read but, as you'll see, it has had a huge impact on the way we live our lives.

We immediately turned the room thermostat on the heating down by one degree, which enables you to burn about 10% less gas or oil. Next we started recycling, well before the wheelie bins were introduced. And the following weekend, I went to the DIY store and bought some wood. I built a compost heap at the end of the back garden for all of the kitchen waste.

From those small beginnings, we've made all sorts of lifestyle and environmental changes. We now have chickens in the back garden, as well as five fruit and veg beds. We used to go camping in my old VW campervan and whilst it's not environmentally friendly from a 'miles per gallon' point of view, you only have to ask yourself how many cars would have been traded in and scrapped during its thirty-seven year life and that fact that all parts are recycled, to realise how environmentally friendly it is! We also go camping for our summer hols and at two music festivals every year.

If I look back, all of these massive changes in the way we live our lives started from that one two minute newspaper article. We changed our consciousness, the way we thought about living our lives.

Changes in Consciousness are often confused with a midlife crisis, it's rarely a crisis! Somebody wakes up one day and asks themselves whether there isn't more to life than this. Their Consciousness, the way they want to live their life, needs to change. Unfortunately, a lot of people, having realised that there's something missing from their lives, then get back on the treadmill and ignore that all important impulse. I often get to see those people six to twelve months later for stress or depression.

Ultimately, if someone is unhappy with the way their life is panning out, they need to step back, get off the treadmill, change their Consciousness and then take action. So many people today are stuck on the treadmill, going to a job they don't enjoy just to pay the bills at the end of the month. That's not living, but our Cultural Programming says that's the way we should be living our lives!

A generation ago, this model worked. We had a job for life. We worked nine till five, took an hour off for lunch, never worked weekends and weren't stressed. You don't need me to point out that that's all changed. Well our Consciousness, the way we think about our lives and the way we live them, needs to change too. We need a new model.

Part of the new Consciousness is that money and possessions aren't what life's about. Our single minded pursuit of success and money needs to stop because it makes very few people genuinely happy.

We need to:

- Get off the treadmill

- Have a good look at our lives

- Work out what makes us happy and what doesn't

- Discuss and make an action plan with our family

- Take action!

We need to change our Consciousness and the decision to do that can be taken in two minutes! Taking the action as a result, is part of life's wonderful ongoing journey. So if you're not happy, get off your damned treadmill!!

The likelihood is that if you, like so many others, realise that something is missing from your life, then you will probably need to make changes at various levels of the ladder, but the important ones occur at the top two levels (Consciousness and Identity). This is why I normally only need to see people for three sessions, even those with seemingly deep issues like depression and eating disorders.

Once they understand The Mind Matrix © and how they are currently creating their unwanted reality, they can change the way they think about themselves (Identity) and the way they think about life (Consciousness). They may then change their Behaviour (but much more easily and quickly now!), their Capability (send themselves on a course, learn a new hobby) or their Environment (get married or divorced), but the important changes happen at Identity or Consciousness level first. The Ladder of Change model offers you a structure to understand where you need to make changes. So get off the treadmill, work out what needs to change and take some action! It is that simple!

Interestingly, you can't make changes to your Identity or Consciousness consciously! If you decided to change your Identity, what would you do? Probably change the way you dress or the way you style your hair. Does that change who you are? No! Obviously not!

Similarly, despite the nature of the word, you can't change your Consciousness consciously either. For example, if as a family we'd made the decision to recycle out of civic duty, how long would we have lasted visiting the 'dump' every week? A couple of months maybe before we got bored? We changed our Consciousness. It wasn't a chore, it was a way of life.

When you understand The Mind Matrix ©, get Self Awareness and Self Esteem, you don't have to use conscious willpower to make changes in your life, they just happen! I often get emails from clients three to six months after coming to see me saying something like: "Oh, you know that change I said I was going to make, Mark? I just realised I made it last week and had to tell you!"

That's because when you go through this process, you fundamentally change your Consciousness, so making changes in Behaviour, Capability or Environment becomes easy. But importantly, you don't need to **try** to change your Identity or your Consciousness, that just happens as part of the process.

Chapter 11:
Neural Recoding ©

> *"You don't need anybody to tell you who you are or what you are. You are what you are!"*
>
> **John Lennon**

I've had this nagging feeling that, for some people, there could be a weak link in The Happiness Hierarchy ©, and that is the movement from Self Acceptance to Self Esteem. This part of the transformation is a very important part of my work with my one to one clients.

Most people, including most readers of this book, don't need and/or don't want to see a therapist. However, many people today are starting to realise that their life isn't working. As you know my dream is to get this understanding 'out there' before somebody gets as far as needing to see a therapist.

Part of moving from Self Acceptance to Self Awareness is leaving stuff from the past behind and committing to changing something in the future. Many of you will simply 'dump your stuff' when you know it's there and will just make a decision and commit to change. Some of you may not be quite there. Your 'stuff' may be slightly bigger, or you may need more Self Esteem/Patience/Courage/Motivation than you currently think you have. But you don't feel the need to see a therapist about it. My worry has been that people in this 'no-man's land' will get the understanding but not make the changes and end up staying where they are.

Eureka! I've got the solution! Now I know that I have the complete answer to help everybody from Self Awareness and onto their journey of Authenticity. Neural Recoding © is the name of the therapy modality I have developed over the last twelve years to help my one to one clients. It involves three four hour sessions as follows:

1.   Understanding: going through The Mind Matrix ©

2.   Dumping Stuff from the Past

3.   Committing to change for the future

Look familiar?! Well Neural Recoding © is a combination of NLP, Life Coaching and Hypnotherapy. Because I've been used to thinking of Neural Recoding © solely as a therapy modality, it had limited reach (i.e. one to one clients only). As soon as I saw it as an educational model, the possibilities opened up.

So I have recorded 'therapy' sessions which you can download from the website and tailor make into your own personal Neural Recoding © session. So for those of you who feel you need a bit of help letting something go and/ or committing to something for the future, you can now download your own solution.

My second and third therapy sessions revolve around the client's own personal 'themes'. You see I don't have a standard Stress session or a standard Anxiety session because everybody does them differently! We have to deal with the 'themes' which are underneath the Stress or Anxiety - anger, grief, Mind Chatter, fear etc.

I have spent many, many hours over the last month going through the last Stress/Anxiety/Depression clients to see what the most common themes were. Apologies for not going through the rest, but a thousand is a good statistically significant sample! The results are listed below (the percentage scores are the percentage of the thousand clients needing that theme):

Introduction and Set Up

- Relaxation (100%)

- Life Changes (100%)

Dumping Stuff from the Past

- Anger (65%)

- Forgiveness (65%)

- Anxiety (55%)

- Saying Goodbye (Grief of losing loved one or getting somebody unloved out of your head!) (40%)

- Mind Chatter (55%)

- Fear of Failure (35%)

- Accept yourself (Dumping Perfectionism) (55%)

Changes for the Future

- Self Esteem (100%)

- Creating a New Beginning (60%)

- Making your Dreams come true (55%)

- Motivation (35%)

- Memory/Concentration (15%)

Summary

- Build up (100%)

- Count Down (100%)

Hypnotherapy

The very word causes so much unnecessary turmoil in many people's minds. Now you know how the Unconscious works and that it can't tell the difference between what you've imagined and what is actually happening to you, it shouldn't come as a great surprise that Hypnotherapy is easily the most effective tool in deleting unwanted emotional and habitual patterns and building new and desired programmes. It is also extremely fast.

Let's just quickly take all of the mystery and drama out of it and debunk the myths in the process.

Hypnosis is extremely simple and easy to achieve. Its sole objective is to take the Conscious, rational, analytical Mind temporarily out of the way. The Unconscious (where all the problems are) is then completely available to be communicated with.

So how do we do that? Well, it's all about being physically very relaxed, because when you're physically very relaxed, three things happen:

- Your breathing rate slows down because you're lying or sitting nice and still and you don't need to gasp in the oxygen

- Your heart rate slows down because you're not moving around and don't need to rush the blood round the system

- Finally and most importantly, your brainwave activity slows down

- Those three things are in what's called a cybernetic loop, which means if one of them slows down, then the others HAVE to follow. If you think about it, you can't have a nice slow breathing rate and your heart going like the clappers! Equally true, but slightly less obvious, you can't have a nice slow breathing (or heart rate) and your Mind racing at 200mph!

So the first part of any hypnosis session is helping you relax physically. It's that dozy feeling when you wake up on a Sunday morning without the alarm clock or when you're dozing on the beach or on the patio. And that's it! Now because it's that simple, people make 3 basic mistakes in terms of what they're expecting, because of the urban myths or what they've seen on TV:

- People expect to know when they're hypnotised. Sorry, you won't have a clue. It's just being nice and relaxed. There's no magic signal that pops up in your head: "Hey Fred, you're now hypnotised!" You're not going to know, so don't worry about it.

- People expect to have fingers snapped at them so that they instantly fall asleep. No, that's not what happens! It takes a good fifteen to twenty minutes to get somebody sufficiently relaxed. However, the problem is that people perceive they can hear what's being said to them. That's fine! You can be perfectly relaxed and still hear. Hypnosis does not equal sleep! So if you can hear the session, that's fine.

- Some people get the opposite problem: "Oh no I fell asleep. I've got to listen to everything he says or it won't work!" Which part of the Mind does the listening?

Hearing is OK, listening is not, subtle difference! Yes, the Conscious Mind! If you think about it, at night you're asleep. Your Conscious Mind is asleep with you, but you're still breathing, blinking and dreaming. Your Unconscious (which is the bit we need to talk to) is active 24 hours a day, otherwise you'd die in your sleep! So don't worry about falling asleep.

The key is don't <u>actively</u> listen to what's being said and if your Mind wants to wander off, let it! Most people's Minds wander in and out. They hear some bits and not others, which is why if they listen to a CD for a second time somebody will quite often think "ooh, didn't hear that bit last time!" Their Mind had simply wandered off in that part the last time they listened. So being in hypnosis is anywhere between being nice and relaxed, but being able to hear, and being asleep. That's a pretty wide spectrum of experiences which all add up to hypnosis. It's almost impossible to not do it properly!

I would always suggest lying down, being covered by a blanket, making sure your head and neck are comfortably supported. I would also suggest you use headphones. Just like when listening to music, it's a much richer listening experience and much easier for the Unconscious to get involved.

So the bottom line is that Hypnosis is a piece of cake! The only people who can't do it, either don't want it or are incapable of relaxing ever. You may be thinking you're not great at relaxing but <u>everybody</u> can relax with a bit of help!

Logistics

Each theme listed above is a separate mp3 file which you can download onto your iPod or P.C. Each track will start with music with the volume building until my voice starts and then fades out at the end. All you need to do is decide which 'themes' you need, decide on the order and download them one after another onto your iPod or P.C. There will be a split second break in the music between each track, but you'll be too relaxed to notice.

Every session should include the Relaxation and Life Changes tracks at the beginning and finish with Build up and then Count Down at the end. I would also suggest that every session starts with Self Esteem just after the Relaxation and Life Changes tracks, since Self Esteem (as you now know) is the key to a better life! In terms of the order for other sessions, it's what feels right, but "Dumping Stuff from the Past' should be first and 'Changes for the Future' should be towards the end.

I would suggest a maximum session length of one hour, maybe one hour ten minutes. The track lengths are listed on the website and each listing has a brief description. You don't need to listen to your session every day for the next ten weeks. There is no particular guideline, although the more you listen to it, the more deeply embedded it will become. If you can listen to it twice the first week and then once each week for the next four weeks, you'll be doing brilliantly. You can then revisit it on an as and when basis.

To access the Neural Recoding © tracks just go to: **www.marknewey.com/neuralrecoding**. And because you've read the book, I'm giving you a 50% discount. Just enter the discount code: *the naked i*. Enjoy! It's probably the most relaxing experience you'll ever have!

Chapter 12:

Over to You!

> "To be nobody-but-yourself in a world which is doing its best, night and day, to make you everybody but yourself – means to fight the hardest battle any human being can fight – and never stop fighting."
>
> **E.E. Cummings**

This is a very short chapter!

Well, now it's your turn. Reading a book will not change your life. Doing the research and the thinking and taking action will!

Chapter 10 The Ladder of Change' will give you food for thought for what action you might need to take in your life, because take action you must!

To take this important work further, please visit **www.marknewey.com** where you will find the following help:

- A free weekly blog with tips for making changes in your life so that you can enjoy life more.

- Free ebooks

- Online courses in Self Awareness, Self Esteem and Authenticity

- Live Workshops on Self Awareness, Self Esteem and Authenticity, as well as Authentic Relationships,

Practices and Rituals for a Happy, Healthy Life, Understanding and enjoying your Emotions, Authentic Warriors (men!) and Authentic goddesses (women!)

- Live Workshops on Creating the Perfect Job, How to be Happy and Successful at Work

- Business Programmes on Leadership, Team, Wellbeing and Corporate Culture Transformation

Please feel free to share your comments, criticisms, discoveries, light bulb moments, changes and progress with me at **mark@marknewey.com**. Feedback allows me to improve what I do. I'm completely open to learning from others for the rest of my life!

Also it allows others, who are currently lost and in need of help to engage with the process and open up to transforming their lives too! This feedback can be part of your actions to make a difference in the world.

Finally, if this book has helped you take a more spiritual look at life and you would like to do your bit to "change the world", it's a lot easier than you think! Look no further than changing yourself. When you are more authentic, happy and fulfilled, you will markedly alter the lives of those around you.

In a groundbreaking piece of research, Christakis and Fowler discovered not only that happiness was contagious, but that there were also effects within social networks. Individuals' happiness was found to be influenced by their position in a social network and by the happiness of those who were closest to them in the network.

They found that the relationship between happy people and their friends who were happy, extended up to three degrees of separation (if you are happy, then you will affect the happiness of your friend's friend's friend!). They concluded that happiness is a 'collective phenomenon' and that the people with whom you have regular physical contact are the people who help determine how happy you are. [1] I like to think of this as changing the world one person at a time!

Be You, Be Happy

Notes

Chapter 2: What is The Mind Matrix ©?

1. **Wax, Ruby.** *Sane New World: Taming The Mind.* Hodder and Stoughton Ltd (2013)

2. **Fine, Cordelia.** *A Mind of Its Own: How your Brain distorts and deceives.* Icon Books Ltd (2007)

3. **Arden, John B.** *Rewire Your Brain: Think Your Way to a Better Life.* John Wiley and Sons (2010)

4. **Miller, George A.** *The Magical Number Seven, Plus Or Minus Two: Some Limits On Our Capacity For Processing Information, why there's a limit to how much information our Minds can process.* Psychological Review (1956)

Chapter 5: Left or Right?

1. **Paul Maclean.** *The Triune Brain in Evolution: Role in Paleocerebral Functions.* Springer (1990)

2. **Pink, Daniel H.** *A Whole New Mind: Why Right-Brainers will rule the Future.* Marshall Cavendish (2008)

Chapter 6: Kids Matter

1. **Dispensa, Joe.** *Evolve your Brain: The Science of Changing Your Mind.* Health Communications (2009)

2. **Ledoux, Joseph.** *Synaptic Self : How Our Brains Become Who We Are.* Penguin (2003)

3. **Sieger, Robin.** *Natural Born Winners: How to Achieve Happiness and Personal Fulfilment.* Arrow Books Ltd (2004)

4. **Dispensa, Joe.** *Evolve your Brain: The Science of Changing Your Mind.* Health Communications (2009)

5. **Laibow, Rima**. *Quantitative EEG and Neurofeedback.* Laibow (1999 and 2002)

6. **Dispensa, Joe.** *Evolve your Brain: The Science of Changing Your Mind.* Health Communications (2009)

Chapter 7: Society Expects...

1. **Godin, Seth.** *Tribes: We Need You to Lead Us.* Piatkus (2008)

2. **James, Oliver.** *Affluenza.* Vermilion (2007)

3. **Tolle, Eckart.** *A New Earth: Create a Better Life.* Penguin (2009)

4. **Griffin, Joe and Tyrrell, Ivan.** *Human Givens: A New Approach to Emotional Health and Clear Thinking.* HG Publishing (2004)

Chapter 8: Is this the Real Life? Is this just Fantasy?

1. **Canfield, Jack.** *How to get From Where You are to Where You want to be: The 25 Success Principles.* Harper Element (2007)

2. **Lucas, Bill.** *rEvolution: How to thrive in crazy Times.* Crown House Publishing (2009)

3. **Arden, John B.** *Rewire Your Brain: Think Your Way to a Better Life.* John Wiley and Sons (2010)

4. **Lipton, Bruce H.** *The Biology of Belief: Unleashing the Power of Consciousness, Matter and Miracles.* Hay House UK (2011)

5. **Lipton, Bruce H.** *The Biology of Belief: Unleashing the Power of Consciousness, Matter and Miracles.* Hay House UK (2011)

Chapter 9: Mental Autopilot

1. **Dispensa, Joe.** *Evolve your Brain: The Science of Changing Your Mind.* Health Communications (2009)

2. **Dispensa, Joe.** *Evolve your Brain: The Science of Changing Your Mind.* Health Communications (2009)

3. **Segal, Williams, Teasdale.** *Mindfulness-Based Cognitive Therapy for Depression: A New Approach to Preventing Relapse.* Guilford Press (2012)

4. **Wax, Ruby.** *Sane New World: Taming The Mind.* Hodder and Stoughton Ltd (2013)

5. **Williams, Teasdale, Segal, Kabat-Zinn.** *The Mindful Way through Depression: Freeing Yourself from Chronic Unhappiness.* Guilford Press (2007)

Chapter 12: Over to You!

1. **Christakis, N.A. and Fowler, J.H.** *Dynamic Spread of Happiness in a Large Social Network: Longitudinal Analysis over 20 Years in the Framlingham Heart Study.* British Medical Journal December (2008)

Resources

Authenticity, Emotions and Health:

- **www.time-to-change.org.uk**

- **www.blackdogtribe.com**

- **TEDx Houston - Brene Brown:**
  www.youtube.com/watch?v=X4Qm9cGRub0

- **TEDxKC - Brene Brown:** *The Price of Invulnerability*
  www.youtube.com/watch?v=_UoMXF73j0c

- **HPI Index:** www.happyplanetindex.org

- **Brown, Brene.** *The Gifts of Imperfection: Let Go of
  Who You Think You're Supposed to Be and Embrace
  Who You Are.* Hazelden Information & Educational
  Services (2010)

- **Brown, Brene.** *Daring Greatly: How the Courage
  to be Vulnerable Transforms the Way We Live, Love,
  Parent, and Lead.* Gotham Books (2012)

- **TedGlobal**
  www.ted.com/talks/ruby_wax_what_s_so_funny_
  about_mental_illness.html

- **Layard Richard.** *Happiness, Lessons from a New
  Science.* Penguin Books (2005)

- **Claire Grant's Cancer blog:**
  www.triplenegative.co.uk/blog

Authenticity and how the Mind works:

- **TED - Sir Ken Robinson: Do schools kill creativity?**
  www.youtube.com/watch?v=jG9CE55wbtY

- **Brain Dominance Profiling:**
  www.mybrain.co.uk

- **Dispensa, Joe.** *Evolve your Brain: The Science of
  Changing Your Mind.* Health Communications (2009)

- **Lipton, Bruce H**. *The Biology Of Belief: Unleashing the Power of Consciousness, Matter and Miracles.* Hay House UK (2011)

- **Hamilton, David.** *How Your Mind Can Heal Your Body.* Hay House UK (2008)

- **Smart, Jamie.** Clarity: *Clear Mind, Better Performance, Bigger Results.* Capstone (2013)

Authenticity, Mindfulness and NLP

- **Mindfulness with John Kabat-Zinn:** www.youtube.com/watch?gl=GB&hl=en-GB&v=3nwwKbM_vJc

- **Mindfulness with Michael Chaskalson:** www.mbsr.co.uk

- **Wax, Ruby.** *Sane New World: Taming The Mind.* Hodder and Stoughton Ltd (2013)

- **Bandler, Richard and Grinder, John.** *Frogs into Princes: Neuro-Linguistic Programming.* Real People Press, U.S. (1981)

Authenticity and Society

- Will's Wisdom (Will Smith): www.youtube.com/watch?v=pSK_Likqv24

- **Godin, Seth.** *Tribes: We Need You to Lead Us.* Piatkus (2008)

- **James, Oliver.** *Affluenza.* Vermilion (2007)

Authenticity and Spirituality:

- **McTaggart, Lynne.** *The Bond: Connecting Through The Space Between Us.* Hay House UK (2011)

- **Tolle, Eckart.** *A New Earth: Create a Better Life.* Penguin (2009)

- **Giser, Art.** www.energeticnlp.com